FLORIDA STATE
UNIVERSITY LIBRARIES

JUN 2 6 2001

TALLAHASSEE, FLORIDA

TALLAHASSEE, FLORIDA

ISRAELI STRATEGY
AFTER DESERT STORM

The Begin-Sadat (BESA) Center for Strategic Studies is dedicated to the study of Middle East peace and security, in particular the national security and foreign policy of Israel. A non-partisan and independent institute, the BESA Center is named in memory of Menachem Begin and Anwar Sadat, whose efforts in pursuing peace laid the cornerstone for future conflict resolution in the Middle East.

Since its founding in 1991 by Dr Thomas O. Hecht of Montreal, the BESA Center has become one of the most dynamic Israeli research institutions. It has developed cooperative relationships with strategic study centres throughout the world, from Ankara to Washington and from London to Seoul. Among its research staff are some of Israel's best and brightest academic and military minds. BESA Center publications and policy recommendations are read by senior Israeli decision-makers, in military and civilian life, by academicians, the press and the broader public.

The BESA Center makes its research available to the international community through three publication series: *BESA Security and Policy Studies, BESA Colloquia on Strategy and Diplomacy* and *BESA Studies in International Security*. The Center also sponsors conferences, symposia, workshops, lectures and briefings for international and local audiences.

Our current research foci are:

- Deterrence and Regional Security
- Israel Defense Forces of the Future
- Israeli Public Opinion on National Security
- Israeli–Turkish Strategic Ties
- Mideast Water Resources
- Middle East Arms Control
- Military Industries
- US–Israel Relations
- Palestinian Positions and Factions in the Peace Process
- Politicians and the Use of Force
- Proliferation and Weapons of Mass Destruction
- Regional Security Régimes
- Space-Based Weaponry
- Strategic Options in the Peace Process
- Terrorism and Low-Intensity Violence

ISRAELI STRATEGY AFTER DESERT STORM

Lessons of the Second Gulf War

AHARON LEVRAN

FRANK CASS
LONDON • PORTLAND, OR.

DS
79.724
I75
L49
1997

First published in 1997 in Great Britain by
FRANK CASS & CO. LTD
Newbury House, 900 Eastern Avenue,
London IG2 7HH

and in the United States of America by
FRANK CASS
c/o ISBS, 5804 N.E. Hassalo Street,
Portland, Oregon 97213-3644, USA

Copyright © 1997 Aharon Levran

British Library Cataloguing in Publication data

A catalogue record for this book is available
from the British Library

ISBN 0-7146-4755-1 (cloth)
ISBN 0-7146-4316-5 (paperback)

Library of Congress Cataloging-in-Publication data

A catalog record for this book is available
from the Library of Congress

*All rights reserved. No part of this publication may be reproduced in any form, or by
any means, electronic, mechanical, photocopying, recording or otherwise, without the
prior permission of Frank Cass and Company Limited.*

Typeset by Regent Typesetting, London
Printed in Great Britain by
Bookcraft (Bath) Ltd, Midsomer Norton, Avon

Contents

Introduction

The Second Gulf War[1] and the Kuwait crisis that preceded it were traumatic events for the Middle East and the entire world. Less than a year had passed since the collapse of the Soviet Union, the West's celebration of its victory over communism, the dissipation of the global tension of the Cold War and what seemed to be the emergence of a 'new world order', when an Arab ruler appeared on the world stage and occupied a smaller neighbouring state. For the first time in the history of the region an Arab country erased another 'sister state' from the map and turned it into a province of its own territory. The far-reaching dangers implicit in this grave development, and Saddam Hussein's cruelty and megalomania, left President of the United States George Bush no option other than to lead a war coalition of some 30 states, including Arab states, against Hussein – the first such event in the history of the Middle East. It is hard to imagine that the United States could have gone to war and assembled such a broad coalition against Saddam if the Soviet Union, Iraq's former patron, had not already collapsed or if the ruler of Iraq had expressed any readiness to reach a settlement.

This war had grave implications for Israel too. For the first time in its history Israel found itself subjected to repeated surface-to-surface missile (SSM) attacks aimed at its civilian population and cities rather than at military targets. It was also the first time Israel had been involved in a war in which it was not a party – a war taking place far from its own soil, and one which put Israel in the embarrassing position of not being able to respond to its aggressors. For the first time in its history, Israel's population was subjected to the fear of attack by chemical (and possibly biological) weapons. For full discussion of the far-reaching strategic and political implications of this it is necessary to obtain a broader picture of Iraq's true non-conventional arsenal. In any event, we have no intention of discussing the strict professional or operational-tactical implications of the war here, nor of analysing the course of its specific operations. Although the professional-operational level is no less militarily important, it is preferable, from an Israeli point of view, to give serious consideration first and foremost to the general picture, namely the strategic features of the war.

Viewing the war from this angle, three features stand out immediately: the SSM attacks against Israel; the war in the air and the display of technological prowess; and the role (or, regrettably, the lack) of intelligence. It is important to analyse the significance to Israel of these three factors, all of which were conspicuous in the war and have far-reaching consequences for future defence posture.

Similarly, two other factors must also be discussed: Saddam Hussein did not use chemical weapons against Israel or the Coalition, and Israel made no response to the repeated SSM attacks on her civilian population. It is important to analyse the impact of these 'non-events' on Israeli strategy and on its deterrence posture.

After such a critical military event as the Second Gulf War, it is always important to assess the risk and possibility of future hostilities erupting between the Arabs and Israel, especially in the wake of the lessons that the states in the region are likely to have learnt from that confrontation. In view of all this, it is necessary to conclude with a discussion of the implications of the Second Gulf War on Israeli defence theory and doctrine.

Still, a qualifying remark is in order: one must bear in mind that even though much has been written and revealed about the war, only a short period has elapsed since the war at the time of writing, and our information and perspective on the subject may not yet be complete.

It is important, however, for Israel to learn the necessary lessons from any war, direct or indirect. This is particularly so in the case of the Second Gulf War since, as has become clear to many, it came to an end too soon – before Iraq's military capability and infrastructure had been sufficiently weakened – and it surely did not succeed in removing Saddam Hussein from the arena. This study does not include an analysis of the unsuccessful conclusion of the war (including the failure to remove Saddam), nor does it analyse its objectives since, in our view, these matters fall into the category of strategic-political issues. Similarly, we don't intend to dwell here on the purely political aspects and consequences of the war, including the Arab–Israeli political process that gathered momentum in the wake of the war. In any event, examination of the military and strategic implications of the war can make us considerably wiser about the residual threats emanating periodically from Iraq, even after the war, and about current strategic developments involving this country and the overall situation in the region.

NOTES

1. As distinguished from the Iran–Iraq war that took place from 1980–88 (the First Gulf War).

1

SSM Attacks on Israel

For the first time in the history of the Arab–Israeli conflict an Arab state made use of surface-to-surface missiles (SSMs) against Israel, and, in particular, against its home front.[1] Previously, Israel's civilian population had indeed faced the risk of Arab fighter planes penetrating its skies, but this menace had been negligible due to the overwhelming superiority of the Israel Air Force (IAF) in general, and certainly in Israeli airspace. In the Second Gulf War, however, Israel's home front was actually its only battlefront. This marked the violation of an unwritten but long-standing rule between Israel and her neighbours that cities and civilian population centres should not be attacked in war. This calls for close analysis of the scope and dimension of the SSM threat against Israel, as well as of ways of coping with it.

SCOPE AND DIMENSION OF THE SSM THREAT AGAINST ISRAEL IN THE WAKE OF THE SECOND GULF WAR

In the Second Gulf War Iraq launched about 40 SSMs at Israel (the number generally cited in public is 39, however there may actually have been as many as 43 missiles) in a total of 17 attacks. The launchings spanned a period of 39 days (from 18 January to 25 February 1991) out of 42 days of battle (17 January–28 February). Although only seven of the 17 missile attacks resulted in loss of life[2] and severe material damage, they nevertheless created a considerable strategic problem for Israel, as could have been expected.[3] Although there was little loss of life, damage and material destruction were significant.

1

Two people were killed in direct strikes and another 11 were killed indirectly, as a result of heart ailments and 'self-protection accidents'. Approximately 1,000 others were affected or wounded, most of them quite mildly.[4] At the same time, over 10,000 apartments and other structures were damaged.[5] Severe to moderate damage was inflicted on a total of 235 structures and 1,250 residential units respectively. Thousands of people were evacuated to hotels from destroyed homes.

It is difficult to precisely estimate the direct and indirect costs to the economy, the greater part of which was paralysed for several weeks. In addition, the educational system and various activities involving large public gatherings were totally shut down. Of course the war incurred special costs on the defence establishment due to the IAF special alert and the increased activity of the intelligence and civil defence services and similar organisations. The American Administration at the time was willing to compensate Israel to the tune of $650 million for the cost of its mobilisation and war damage, even though the total cost of this war for Israel actually came to several billion dollars.[6] Interestingly, a year after the war, a press survey[7] cited a figure of some 5 billion IS (or more than $2 billion), including the cost of direct damage to buildings and property, exceptional costs to the defence establishment, disruption of the economy in manufacturing, construction, export, tourism, agriculture, foreign investment, and air travel, and increased costs for shipping, insurance, fuel, and so forth.

Estimates of possible SSM casualties made before the war, based on the toll taken by Iraq's missile attacks on Teheran in March–April 1988, and adjusted for different conditions in Israel, projected figures of three people killed and seven or eight wounded per missile.[8] Indeed, the number of direct SSM casualties in Israel – approximately 300 (after subtracting casualties due to panic and atropine misuse) – shows that these estimates were generally quite accurate. However, the number of direct and indirect fatalities from SSM attacks on Israel was far lower than in the Iraq–Iran war (1980–88), yet the one successful Iraqi missile strike on an American installation in Daharan (Saudi Arabia) on 27 February 1991, which inflicted a toll of 29 lives and wounded another 90 people (similar to the effect of other successful SSM strikes in the First Gulf War) indicates that the losses in Israel could have been far worse. In any event, although loss of life in Israel was light, material damage was not and it provides concrete evidence of the destructive potential of missiles.

Overall, the impact of the SSM *threat* to Israel was more severe and far-reaching than its *manifestation* in terms of loss of life, material damage and disruption of normal life. The attacks on Israel by Iraqi al-Hussein missiles (Soviet Scud Bs whose range had been doubled to approximately 650 km by reducing the weight of their warheads from one tonne to about 250 kg and by extending their fuselages to add fuel) should be viewed through a broader strategic prism in which psychological and strategic aspects carry great weight. It may be said that, although the SSMs launched at Israel achieved no significant strategic gain, they nevertheless put Israel's national strength and staying-power to the test.

The SSM attacks were traumatic for most Israelis. For the first time in its history, Israel was in the embarrassing position of requiring most of its people to close themselves in hermetically-sealed rooms. Many chose to flee from high-risk areas to more secure regions of Israel and some even fled abroad. The unique circumstances of the war gave rise to a sense of danger and helplessness which lasted several weeks.[9] The axiom that had characterised the public's way of thinking – that the Israeli home front would be safe against substantial threat in time of war – had been disproved, adversely affecting national morale.[10] Nevertheless, throughout the war, the government's policy of restraint received massive public support.[11] There were certainly rational reasons for this – a desire not to grant Saddam's wish of dragging Israel into the war, to leave the work of weakening Israel's enemy to the Coalition, and so forth; however, it may also have reflected a certain lack of resilience, and it certainly revealed the public's readiness not to react to the blows inflicted on the nation (as long as those blows could be perceived as tolerable); in other words, to a large extent, it revealed a population weary of struggle and war and the weakness of Israel's staying power.

It is worth noting that the SSM attacks on Israel occurred under less severe circumstances than the Iraqi SSM attacks on Teheran in 1988. The Iranian population had not received the benefit of five minutes advance warning. In Israel missiles fell only at night, so that after a while the country and its economy were able to return to a more normal way of life, whereas in Iran, by contrast, missiles fell mostly in the daytime, thus causing higher casualties, as well as greater fear and disruption of life. In Teheran most of the missiles (approximately 150) fell in salvos, whereas in Israel the vast majority of them fell singly.[12] More important was the fact that, in the Second Gulf War, the Iraqi missile launchers were hunted from the air by the Coalition's air force, whereas in the war with Iran the Iraqi missile launchers operated without any impediment. Israel probably had fewer casualties because of these differences but her population still suffered a psychological impact.

The SSM attacks posed an acute strategic problem for Israel for three reasons: the lack of a specific military-technological countermeasure against missile attacks; the US politically blocking Israel from launching an offensive option to cope with the missile threat; and the embarrassing situation of Israel's population being subject to missile attack without the Israel Defence Force (IDF) fighting at the front. In other words, despite their singularity, the SSM attacks were indeed meaningful for Israel.

Israel was attacked by ballistic missiles at a time when no specific appropriate, military-technological response to such a threat existed anywhere in the world. This does not mean that SSMs are absolute weapons with no technology to counter them. We are currently in a period of transition, at the end of which an appropriate countermeasure will be found, developed and deployed; for this is the historical dialectic of weapons development. Recall that, in the Lebanese war (1982), Israel demonstrated an effective solution for the problem of coping with the threat of surface-to-air missiles (SAMs), a substantial menace to its air force which first seriously emerged in the Yom Kippur War (1973). Ironically, in 1973, too, some 'wise' experts maintained that the missile had twisted the airplane's tail and even went so far as to predict that fixed-wing aircraft would soon be obsolete.

The seriousness of Israel's position, and the condition of its national morale during the Second Gulf War, were worsened due to the political constraints placed on her by her ally, the United States, whose sensitivity about preserving the Coalition intact (especially with regard to its Arab partners) bordered on extremism. These constraints prevented Israel from invoking the offensive option at her disposal to counter the source of the threat – the SSM disposition in western Iraq – or from attacking Iraq's infrastructure. Before the war broke out Israel had been planning to eliminate, or at least neutralise, the Iraqi SSM threat by means of its offensive option – specifically by using its air force in conjunction with ground units. But since the IDF lacked special technological countermeasures, and since the offensive option was not available due to political constraints, Israel found itself helpless in the face of repeated SSM attacks.

Israel's distress was deepened by the fact that its population had become a hostage and a punching-bag for Saddam Hussein in a war in which Israel was not party and which was being fought far from its borders and under unique circumstances. If the IDF had been involved in active fighting on the front, or even if Israel had struck back at Iraq, the impact made by the SSMs would surely have faded in the din of battle and the matter would have been perceived in a different way by the public. But when a considerable proportion of Israel's population had to bear the brunt of SSM strikes alone, it is no wonder that fear of the missile threat, and perhaps even fear for Israel's overall security, were greatly magnified. The sense of hardship and embarrassment were further aggravated by Israel's failure to deter Iraq since deterrence has always been a crucial pillar of Israel's security doctrine and posture.

Be that as it may, SSM attacks on Israel did not pose a threat to its survival. The missiles did not create a situation which could be viewed as an unbearable threat to the country in terms of physical conquest or the destruction of its power centres. We were not dealing with weapons that were particularly militarily decisive or effective, thus posing an intolerable threat to Israel's existence. In fact, Saddam's only strategic response in the war was to launch SSMs – essentially a feeble response. Firing missiles at Israel did not even succeed in drawing her into the war, as Saddam probably desired. Missiles alone cannot win wars, and they certainly cannot determine their outcome, just as fire power alone cannot do so in conventional warfare. Saddam could have fired all his missiles on Kuwait, and still he would not have succeeded in conquering one inch of her soil, or of Saudi soil (see the discussion in Chapter 7).

It should be noted that the above discussion pertains to conventional SSMs landing on a civilian home front, and not to missiles with non-conventional warheads or conventional SSMs fired with great accuracy at sensitive military objectives. Summing up the discussion thus far, we can make the following observations:

- The Israeli home front is no longer immune to enemy attack, especially by missiles.

- Even though Iraq's missile attacks were not strategically successful, their strikes on the Israeli population had a severe psychological impact, whether due to the shock of their first occurrence or the unique circumstances of these attacks.

- SSMs are weapons easily employed by a country that either has inferior air power or is reluctant to risk what air power it has. The purpose of these weapons might be to wear down enemy resilience by significant physical, and especially psychological, harassment.

- Today, in contrast to the past, Israel faces a threat of fire power launched from distant countries having no common border with her.

- Missiles alone cannot produce victory, and most probably will not be able to win wars, just as fire power alone cannot determine the victor in conventional warfare. On the other hand, missiles, in contrast to other components of military might, are quite easy to employ.

- In the final analysis, the cost of missile attacks in damage and loss of life is not intolerable; but this depends on the resolve of the population hit and the circumstances of the strikes. The overall impact on Israel, including the psychological anxiety as well as some of the general damage, also stemmed from the apprehension (which proved unfounded) that Saddam would use chemical weapons.

In short, the SSM threat was not negligible, as various military leaders tried to portray it before the war and, regrettably, also after the war.[13] It is certainly a strategic threat, although it may be of little importance from a strictly military point of view.

In the future, SSMs may well become a greater threat to Israel in the light of the lessons the Arab states in the region might learn from the Second Gulf War. These states are likely to be impressed by the great damage and potent effect that simple surface-to-surface missiles were able to inflict on Israel. Well before the Second Gulf War, most of the Arab states viewed SSMs as a force equaliser countering the proven superiority of the IAF over their own air forces. The Syrian Scud C deal with North Korea, for example, was concluded well before the Second Gulf War (in 1989), although delivery of the missiles did not begin until after the war. Similarly, Syria's negotiations for M-9 surface-to-surface missiles from China (the outcome of which is not yet clear) were initiated before the war.

In any event, the present and the developing Syrian SSM disposition appear more threatening to Israel than the Iraqi missile arsenal in the Second Gulf War because of the greater weight of the original warheads of the Scud B (approximately 1 tonne), the greater accuracy of the missiles, especially the SS-21 (capable of hitting military point targets within an accuracy of 50–100 metres), and the large number of chemical warheads (several hundred) on their Scuds. The Syrian SSM threat has been substantially increased by their recent acquisition of Scud Cs together with the technology for producing them in Syria.

In general the Arabs view SSMs not only as a force equaliser, but also as a means of striking at distant targets (a so-called 'long-arm' capability). Israel's attacks into Egypt in the War of Attrition (1969–70) and its strategic attacks into Syria in the Yom Kippur War (1973) led the Arabs to conclude that they needed to possess an appropriate response in order to deter Israel, especially since their own air forces did not seem to have the capability to carry out attacks deep into Israel.[14] The Second Gulf War is bound to lead the Arabs to conclude that SSMs can offset Israel's qualitative superiority, at least as long as there is no adequate countermeasure for coping with missiles. They will therefore undoubtedly continue attempting to increase the quantity of their SSM arsenal and improve its quality in terms of such factors as range, accuracy, warheads, and manoeuvrability.

Improved SSMs would offer the Arabs greater flexibility of action and would threaten sensitive Israeli military targets such as airfields, headquarters, and war-reserve store units (POMCUS), especially during the critical initial hours of a war when Israel would need the full and unimpaired might of its air force and would have to ensure a smooth and orderly call-up of its reserve formations. A similar, serious strategic implication of such SSMs is that they might hamper the Israeli air force from operating strategically deep in enemy territory – a measure that would aim, *inter alia*, at shortening the duration of a war under favourable conditions. At the same time, the Arabs could disrupt Israel's morale and capacity for a military response, thus helping them to achieve their political objectives with greater ease.

Moreover, long range SSMs, including the al-Hussein, the Scud C, and the M-9 (as opposed to the original Scud B with its intermediate range of 300 km), are certainly not an easy challenge for Israel to meet, let alone longer-range SSMs.

Missiles with a range of some 600 km will give Arab armies, first and foremost Syria, better coverage of targets throughout Israel. More significantly, the Arabs, especially the Syrians, will be able to operate such missiles from deep within their territory, thus making IDF offensive operation against the missiles more difficult and thereby increasing their ability to survive counter attacks. The task of removing the missile threat is therefore likely to become much more complex for Israel.

An even greater strategic challenge for Israel will be to cope with missile launchings from distant countries, both Arab and Moslem. Until the Second Gulf War, Arab states and other states in the 'second circle' could participate in wars against Israel mainly by dispatching expeditionary forces and by sending back-up arms and munitions to the 'first-circle' states, as Iraq, Saudi Arabia, Libya, Kuwait, Morocco and other countries had done in the past. In the Second Gulf War, Israel witnessed a new and significant development – it became prey to fire from a distant Arab state. Almost the only way in which such a distant state could achieve this was by firing SSMs – a relatively easy military task in contrast to the task of dispatching fighter jets, which is far more risky and could easily result in failure. Moreover, a distant SSM aggressor is likely to feel immune from IDF retaliation due to the great distance. This is, therefore, without doubt a new and acute strategic threat and challenge for Israel.

The scope of this threat in practice has broadened with attempts by Iran and Libya to acquire or develop an arsenal of long-range missiles reaching 1,000 km or more and capable of striking Israel. Iran is in the process of acquiring recently-developed No-Dong-1 missiles from North Korea with a range of about 1,200 km. If the efforts of Iran and other states are not forestalled they may be in possession of long-range missiles soon. It is worth recalling that Saudi Arabia has already purchased some CSS-2 SSMs from China with a range of approximately 2,500 km, although no more than a few dozen at this stage. Most importantly, the SSM threat is likely to take on a non-conventional dimension. Iraq has already acknowledged possession of dozens of chemical warheads for its missiles and, as we have mentioned, similar warheads also exist in Syria's missile arsenal.

In conclusion, the scope and dimension of the SSM threat against Israel in the future will depend, *inter alia*, on the following factors: first, on maintaining current international sanctions against, and supervision of, Iraq; second, on invoking international measures to curb missile proliferation, such as the Missile Technology Control Régime (MTCR) of 1987 and the Bush initiative of 29 May 1991, calling for the elimination of missiles with a range of more than 150 km in the context of a regional arms control regime.[15] Realisation of these measures, however, is extremely complex and depends greatly on the goodwill of various suppliers (such as North Korea and China), and, not surprisingly, on rising unemployment among all suppliers (including the United States itself). It depends especially on the willingness of radical clients in the region, including Iran, Libya and Syria, to show restraint in the acquisition and use of missiles and armaments. Third, the threat will be a function of the development capabilities of the states in the region. One way of circumventing a possible international embargo is to produce missiles indigenously, or to convert existing missiles to attain longer ranges and better performance. It is not, therefore, surprising that Syria and Iran purchased their Scud C missiles from Korea together with production lines and technology. This will enable them to convert the missiles to longer ranges than the original, as Iraq converted its Scud B missiles into al-Husseins with twice the range. One cannot, therefore, expect the SSM threat in the Middle East to be curbed or to subside in the near future.

COPING WITH THE SSM THREAT

In the Second Gulf War, Saddam Hussein attacked Israel with impunity. This is not a healthy situation for a country embroiled in a bitter and prolonged conflict with hostile neighbours. Israel cannot afford to be in a situation where it has no adequate response to continually arising threats to her security. Just as the IDF found successful ways of neutralising the surface-to-air missile (SAM) threat to its air force, so too must Israel hasten to find a proper remedy to the threat of SSMs aimed at her population and at sensitive targets. Moreover, the more heavily Arab states rely on SSMs as their 'long arm' and as their answer to Israeli air supremacy, the more the IDF must prove that 'whatever you can do, I can do better'. This is, after all, the crux of any strategic confrontation. It is, after all, what characterised the recent victory of the West over the communist bloc (the US Strategic Defense Initiative (SDI) or "Star Wars" programme seems to have been the straw that broke the camel's back).

The Second Gulf War illustrated the three basic options for coping with SSMs: passive defence; offence; and active defence. There is no point here in dealing in detail with passive defence, by which we refer to the protection of the population by traditional measures such as shelters, protected spaces, and hermetically-sealed rooms. Of course this option should be improved, subject to Israel's financial means. Given Israel's limited financial resources, however, it is hard to foresee any revolutionary improvements in this field. One measure that has been adopted was to establish the Home Front Command and to increase the population's awareness of protective measures. On the whole, this option remains essentially defensive and passive, and *ipso facto* cannot yield the necessary strategic results such as winning a war or determining its outcome.

The offensive option, on the other hand, which essentially encompasses an air and/or land attack on the disposition of SSM launchers either prior to or during an actual missile threat, was and remains the principal countermeasure for Israel (and other countries) even in the era of political settlements. Yet the operational difficulties of this option had been foreseen,[16] and the Second Gulf War only provided further evidence reinforcing this observation. Even though the Coalition's air force ruled Iraqi skies, their success in destroying or neutralising missile launchers was quite minimal.

According to UN Security Council Resolution 687 (3 April 1991), Iraq had to report on her remaining stockpiles of non-

11

conventional weapons and SSMs. Accordingly, on 20 April 1991, Iraq reported that it still had 52 al-Hussein missiles (and more later on), but more importantly, that it had ten mobile launchers of all types and 28 stationary launchers, all the stationary ones and four of the mobile ones being located in western Iraq.[17] Of particular interest to us is the number of mobile launchers, especially for al-Hussein missiles (since the original Scud Bs could not reach Israel).

Before and during the war, American and Israeli intelligence estimated that Iraq had a total of 28–30 stationary launchers (all positioned in western Iraq), and, more importantly, approximately 30 mobile Scud launchers of all sorts.[18] These included both original mobile Scud B launchers that had been converted into custom-designed al-Hussein mobile launchers, and towed launchers developed in Iraq and specifically configured for these missiles. The total of 30 mobile launchers also included some original mobile Scud B launchers which had been purchased with the original missiles but were apparently less suitable for launching missiles at Israel. In the final analysis, it was estimated that 8–12 mobile al-Hussein launchers were deployed in western Iraq; this was approximately half of the al-Hussein launchers (the other half being aimed at Saudi Arabia, at which approximately 45 such missiles were fired during the war). Indeed, the largest salvo fired at Israel (on 18 January 1991) consisted of eight missiles, perhaps reflecting deployment of a missile regiment generally comprised of eight to 12 launchers. Assuming that the intelligence estimates were based on sound information and that Iraq generally falsified reports on the quantity of weaponry remaining in her possession, clearly the offensive option failed to destroy the launchers – especially the mobile ones.

Obviously attacks on fixed-site launchers were relatively more successful. It seems that some 12 launchers were hit,[19] but they were of secondary importance in actual missile launching and apparently served as decoys and as a reserve for the mobile launchers. Attempts to destroy mobile launchers, by contrast, were virtually all unsuccessful.[20] According to several reliable sources, including a noted American researcher (Professor Marvin Miller of the Massachusetts Institute of Technology), not a single mobile launcher was destroyed. A much more authoritative source, *The Air Force's Gulf War Survey*, released in May 1993, affirms that the survey did not, in fact, discover hard evidence of the destruction of any mobile missiles.[21] To the best of our knowledge, hardly any of the mobile launchers were hit at all. Undoubtedly General Schwarzkopf's report on 20 January 1991, that 30 stationary launchers and approximately 16 mobile launchers had been destroyed, appears, at best, to have been mistaken. Even the Pentagon spokesman took pains at the time to respond immediately to Professor Miller's article and admitted that not many launchers had been destroyed.[22] Yet, well before the Air Survey's statement was made public, this spokesman added that the number of mobile launchers destroyed was unknown. A very important remark in this regard was made by Rolf Ekeus, head of the UN Special Commission (UNSCOM) charged with the task of ensuring that Iraq dismantled all weapons of mass destruction and the means of delivering them: 'In all the bombing, hardly any of the Scud missiles and launchers were destroyed.'

American aircraft undoubtedly had a serious problem locating and eliminating small and evasive targets such as SSM launchers. This was, after all, the first time in the history of war that SSM launchers had been attacked from the air. Interestingly, the lack of success in this campaign also extended to the special forces (Delta and SAS) employed in western Iraq towards the end of the war. The very fact of these forces being put into action points to the limited success of the air battle. The height of ridiculousness was reached in the story, published on 27 February 1991, lauding these special forces for destroying no fewer than 26 SSM launchers. This implied that such a large number of launchers was still in operation one day before the end of the war, even after so many had already been destroyed.[23]

This is not to say that the United States' effort was entirely futile nor that its air force did not try to stop SSMs from being fired at Israel, as Major General E. Ben-Nun, then Commander of the Israel Air Force, maintained.[24] In support of his charge, Ben-Nun cited the small number of sorties the US made in the region – 'only about 3,000 flights out of a total of 118,000 sorties[25] made in the course of the war' – in other words, approximately 2.5 per cent of the total flights (or somewhat more assuming that fewer than half were actual air strikes).[26] The difficulty, however, was not so much a matter of intention and amount of effort as a matter of poor American performance in coping with SSMs. Nevertheless, the air campaign against the SSMs in western Iraq was far from futile. The very fact that the Iraqi missile force was constantly harassed from the air and could not operate freely in daylight reduced its efficacy. The effect was felt in the considerable decrease in the rate of missile attacks from there: in the first ten days of the war, 26 missiles were fired at Israel; only 14 missiles, mostly launched singly, were fired in the following 33 days of the war. The chase after the missiles from the air also forced the Iraqis to move their launchers from one site to another. The net effect was to markedly reduce the number of missiles fired at Israel and to disperse their impact throughout the country, ultimately lowering the rate of al-Hussein attacks. Thus, the problem in America's handling of the missile menace was more the inability of its air force to hit point targets than a lack of desire to devote sufficient military effort to the matter.

The Israel Air Force, in contrast, might have been more successful in the battle against SSM launchers in western Iraq (in terms of destroying or neutralising them) for several reasons. First, the IAF gained substantial experience in a very similar situation when it dealt with great (and, at the time, surprising) success with the Syrian disposition of SAMs on the Syrian–Lebanese border in the Lebanese War (1982). Second, the IAF was better prepared – operationally, doctrinally and in terms of special weaponry – to cope with a missile threat, since this was its primary mission in this war. Third, since SSMs were the principal national concern for Israel and her inhabitants, the IAF was probably better prepared for this mission in terms of motivation and willingness to take risks. Fighting the missile disposition in western Iraq was a secondary issue for the US.

General Schwarzkopf even compared it to a 'thunderstorm in Georgia'.[27]

Even after the war former IAF Commander Ben-Nun was sure *that the Scuds could have been stopped by employing special techniques both from the air and on the ground.*[28] Since the matter was never put to the test, his assertion remains unproved. This is because the Israeli offensive option was precluded politically, and because, to put it mildly, combat conditions for operations in western Iraq were not favourable to the IAF. The difficulties facing the IAF included geographical distance, real-time intelligence gathering and operational control, passing through Jordanian and/or Saudi air-space and co-ordination with Coalition aircraft. Nevertheless, former Minister of Defence Moshe Arens asserted that Israel had even been prepared to send in ground units to locate the SSMs if attempts to fight them had continued with limited success.[29] There is good reason to believe that this and other ways and means would have increased Israel's chances of neutralising the Iraqi SSMs – or many of them.

Consequently, when Israel first realised that a situation could develop in which it would be prevented from implementing its offensive option, either as a pre-emptive strike or as a means of suppressing a missile threat, and when it became clear that the American anti-missile offensive had not been successful, the third option, 'active defence', became much more important. Active defence is characterised by the ability to intercept SSMs in flight, preventing them from reaching their target. The technology for this, first and foremost anti-missile missiles (ATBMs), is currently under development both in Israel and the US.

In the Second Gulf War an embryonic system of active defence was employed: the Patriot Pac-2. This system appeared to have a very limited capability for intercepting missiles in flight. The Patriot, however, was not originally designed for this purpose, and therefore was not effective against SSMs. (Originally Patriots were intended to serve as advanced anti-aircraft SAMs, but in the mid-1980s some missile-interception capability was added.) The shortcomings of the Patriot in countering al-Hussein missiles can be summarised in three points. First, the Patriot was not suitable for intercepting converted Scuds having twice the range and flying at a greater velocity. Second, the tendency of al-Hussein missiles to break up in the air (as we have mentioned, these were Iraqi-made improvisations) posed critical problems for interception by Patriots, such as distinguishing the missile's warhead from other less important parts. If the Patriots had been intercepting original Scud B missiles or short-range SS-21 missiles, presumably they would have been more successful. Third, the shortcoming of the Patriot system was most evident in its missile point-interception capability; it possessed a limited defence perimeter and rather low altitude interception. More than once this caused superfluous collateral damage and even deflected an SSM into the defended area.[30]

Exaggerated and misleading reports were circulated with regard to the Patriot's performance in the Second Gulf War, especially by the Raytheon company involved in its production, and the US Army.[31] At first Raytheon maintained that the Patriots intercepted SSMs with 90 per cent success in Saudi Arabia and 50 per cent success in Israel. By contrast, Israeli experts were hard pressed to find more than one or two instances in which the Patriots intercepted an al-Hussein warhead and they found no reason for assuming that the performance was much different in Saudi Arabia. The Pentagon had to change its version regarding the Patriot's success in the war, just as it had to change its figures for destruction of SSM launchers. In a subsequent report to Congress, the US Army claimed that the Patriots successfully intercepted only 40 per cent of the SSMs fired at Israel and 70 per cent of those fired at Saudi Arabia, where interception was defined as exploding the warhead or deflecting it from its target.

Irrespective of the reliability of these reports, the Patriots deserve praise for proving, for the first time in the history of warfare, that it is possible to intercept SSMs in flight – and this is no mean feat. Thus, with all their limitations, the Patriots proved that the notion of active defence is valid.[32] The improved Patriot Pac-3 system, currently under development,[33] is likely to be more effective in terms of encountering and destroying the target, and intercepting at a higher altitude and greater distance (approximately 20 km) from the defended area. It still remains, however, a system primarily designed for point defence.

The Arrow (Hetz) system, developed in Israel with American co-operation and mostly American financing as part of the SDI programme, has, by contrast, been designed from the outset to provide optimal defence against advanced SSMs (with ranges exceeding 1,000 km), including missiles with non-conventional warheads, intercepting them at very high altitudes (above 40 km) and long ranges (more than 100 km). One of the main advantages planned for the Arrow is an extremely high velocity (approximately Mach 8), enabling it to operate as a multi-layer system, capable of firing more than one Arrow at a single target. Nevertheless, numerous problems have been encountered in developing such a technologically ambitious system. The first three experimental runs of the missile failed. Additional tests were more successful and guaranteed continued American financial support. However, several years are likely to pass before the entire system becomes operational.

With respect to active defence, other countermeasures are being developed as well as the Arrow. The US is in the process of developing the Erint and Theater High Altitude Area Defense (THAAD) systems, and the Patriot Pac-3 point-defence system mentioned above. Both the US and Israel are developing collateral systems such as high-velocity guns (HVGs) and remote-piloted vehicles (RPVs). While high-speed guns are intended to provide another point-defence system against missiles that manage to penetrate the Arrow multi-layer defence, RPVs are based on a different concept. Under certain very specific circumstances RPVs might provide Israel with an alternative to ATBMs, such as the Arrow, since they have the capability to detect and possibly destroy SSMs in their more vulnerable initial stage of flight.

Of course the traditional questions of cost-effectiveness and the allocation of financial resources have arisen with respect to the Arrow project. With regard to cost-effectiveness, there are those who challenge the wisdom of intercepting an SSM whose cost is rather inexpensive by an anti-missile missile that costs several times as much. But the fact is that even the 'primitive' al-Hussein missiles were quite expensive, costing several hundred thousand dollars each. Two factors account for this high price: first, the costliness of the original Scud B missile itself (despite unfounded claims to the contrary) and, second, the fact that to produce each al-Hussein missile, the Iraqis had to cannibalise two original Scud B missiles.

Furthermore, price should not be the main criterion in weighty strategic considerations. The correct criterion ought to be an assessment of the damage that an SSM with a conventional or non-conventional warhead can inflict on the strength and staying-power of a country, coupled with the cost in terms of loss of life, material damage, and disruption to daily living. Besides, the Patriot missiles were not much cheaper than the projected Arrow missiles ($750,000 for a Patriot as compared to an anticipated $1,000,000 for an Arrow), and were certainly more expensive than the al-Hussein. Yet few, if any, people questioned why dozens of them were fired at the al-Hussein missiles (and rightly so).[33] Moreover, one must bear in mind that the cost of this war to Israel, under the most conservative estimates, was assessed to be more than $2 billion.

Incidentally, the cost-effectiveness question can be reduced to absurdity. If SSMs or, for that matter, even a nuclear bomb were given free to an enemy country, should that have a bearing on the strategic considerations, including the issue of cost-effectiveness, which are valid for the defending party?

With respect to the financial resources required for the Arrow programme, one must distinguish between the stage of *development*, which may total some $480 million, the vast part (currently 72 per cent and previously 80 per cent) of which is financed by the United States, and the stage of *production and deployment*, which may exceed $2 billion (over several years), depending on the extent of the IDF's procurement plan. Aside from advanced missiles and launchers, the system is expected to include a radar system capable of detecting missiles at ranges of about 1,000 km, making it possible to provide several minutes 'advance warning'. Moreover, the Arrow project will include fire-control radars and command systems. The fire-control radars are capable of detecting incoming missiles at several hundred kilometres and provide a reasonable back-up for the larger detecting radar system, whose fate is still uncertain. It should be noted that Israel does not have the necessary resources to finance a satellite for early warning of SSM attacks (the Israeli Ofeq satellites are not intended for this purpose). The question of resource allocation touches a sensitive nerve: at the expense of what other military needs will this project be developed? It is not surprising that criticism of the Arrow comes primarily from IAF circles, who assume they will bear the brunt of the expense. To their credit, it must be said that their arguments against the Arrow do not merely focus on resource allocation but also on a difference of perception: is it correct, they ask, to invest in a one-dimensional defensive system instead of in versatile and offensive weapons systems? (See the discussion in Chapter 7.)

It is worth mentioning here that at the end of April 1996 President Clinton decided to proceed with the third phase of the deployment of the Arrow missile programme and committed the US to another $200 million.[34] This followed the signing of a joint US–Israeli Statement of Intent (SOI) on theatre missile defence co-operation. The SOI thus reaffirms US support for Israel's efforts to develop a defence against ballistic missiles as well as for the Arrow deployment programme (ADP), which will conclude the development of this system. Moreover, this SOI will also ensure that Israel's ATBM defences are integrated with US theatre capabilities and enhance interoperability (including provision of early warning launchings). All this no doubt attests to two significant points: first, that the Arrow programme, with all its difficulties, proceeds well, and is a promising ATBM system, and secondly, that the US is willing to take a larger part in it.

There are critics who argue (rather strangely) that an active defence system (such as the Arrow) will prove to be a destabilising factor in the region and will accelerate the arms race there.[35] This, however, cannot be a sound argument.

Surface-to-surface missiles today pose a major strategic challenge to Israel, certainly no less than a 'regular war' (which is primarily a matter of manoeuvres and movements of massive forces). To tell Israel not to meet this challenge properly, for fear that doing so will eliminate the advantage of the other side or will thus increase instability in the region, is at best a peculiar argument. When the Arab states acquired SSMs in order to cope with IAF superiority, few voices vociferously protested that they were increasing regional instability or stepping up the arms race and upsetting the balance of power. In fact, the Arabs did not budge in the least from their plans for a military build-up. Moreover, regional stability will only be strengthened when players like Saddam in the Middle East understand that they cannot threaten others with terroristic weapons systems. Surface-to-surface missiles are essentially destabilising weapons, and the sooner a remedy to them exists the better.

Lastly, a similar argument was raised in the early 1980s against the American SDI programme. If anything is to be given credit for contributing decisively to the collapse of the Soviet empire and bringing the Cold War to an end, it was precisely this programme. Furthermore, in the wake of the Second Gulf War the United States launched the Global Protection Against Limited Strikes programme, designed to neutralise the SSM threat from any corner of the world, and Israel has been invited to participate.

The importance of active defence transcends the interesting questions discussed above. Even though the IDF certainly has unique and effective methods for coping with SSM dispositions, it is highly doubtful whether the offensive option can obtain full success due to objective handicaps such as distance and weather. The more distant the origin of a threat, the harder for an air force to deal with it effectively; and weather has always been, and still remains, enemy number one for any air force.

In the future the offensive option will encounter additional limitations in the form of advanced anti-aircraft missile systems, such as the SAM-10 and the like – the parallel

Soviet version of the American Patriot missile – which will add considerably to the difficulty of gathering air intelligence and carrying out IAF operations on a continuous basis, especially many hundreds of kilometers from home. Moreover, if the IDF has to cope with a number of enemies and threats simultaneously, it will also face a crucial problem in terms of the ratio of forces and ordering its operational priorities (whom to fight first, and with what force). This is especially true in view of its diminishing order of battle (ORBAT) in the air and on the ground. Even if the IAF could have destroyed the SSMs in western Iraq more successfully than the Americans, this would not have guaranteed success in the future, since the IAF would have been operating there after Coalition aircraft had defeated the Iraqi air force and had suppressed its air defence system.

Adding the dimension of active defence will strengthen the IDF's deterrent posture in several respects:

(a) there will no longer be a sense of vulnerability in the face of SSM attack;

(b) there will be another option and greater flexibility in coping with the threat;

(c) it will help neutralise Arab strategy, which relies so heavily on SSMs as a long-range weapon;

(d) most important of all, this option will also make it possible to cope with very long-range SSMs – missiles having a range exceeding 500–600 km, which are likely to appear in the arena soon. The IDF will not be able to cope systematically with long-range SSMs (1,200 km) nor deal effectively with any distant country in the region that might attack Israel by means of offensive action. Hence, active defence must be viewed as no less important than the option of offence.

In conclusion, the lessons of the Second Gulf War with respect to SSMs do not leave Israel many options. In order to cope with the missiles that exist in the Middle East at present, and with the more dangerous ones that will exist in the future,

Israel must have suitable military answers soon. These must be flexible and varied, since one cannot rely on a single option alone. Specifically, Israel must focus on two options simultaneously: offensive capability, and active defence. If there is a central lesson for Israel to learn from employment of SSMs in the Second Gulf War, it is the importance of active defence. In response to the argument that the Arrow cannot assure 100 per cent successful interception – which is particularly crucial in dealing with non-conventional SSMs – one must remember that almost no weapon system can do so. Even a system which is less than perfect can, however, deter the enemy from launching non-conventional weapons for there is no assurance that the weapon launched will not fall into the high percentage of sure interceptions (expected to be around 99 per cent for the Arrow), and that afterwards the enemy may be at the mercy of the country it has attacked and which may deliver a devastating counter-strike.

NOTES

1. In the Yom Kippur War (1973), some of the two dozen or so Frog rockets launched by Syria also hit surrounding civilian settlements, although their target was the Ramat David airfield. Cf. J. S. Bermudez, 'The Syrian Missile Threat', *Marine Corps Gazette*, January 1985.
2. Cf. 'Israel in the Gulf War', *Ma'ariv*, 29 March 1991, p. 41 (hereafter *Ma'ariv Report*).
3. A. Levran, *The Threat of SSMs to Israel*, [Hebrew], Memorandum No. 24, Jaffee Center for Strategic Studies, Tel Aviv University, July 1988 (hereafter, Levran, *SSM Memo*); A. Levran, 'Threats facing Israel from SSMs', *IDF Journal*, No. 19, Winter 1990; A. Levran, 'The Growing Threat to Israel's Rear', *The Middle East Military Balance 1987–1988*, (Jaffee Center for Strategic Studies, Tel Aviv University, 1988).
4. 'Report of the Chief Medical Officer to the IDF', *Ma'ariv*, 29 March 1991.
5. *Ma'ariv*, 17 May 1991; *Jerusalem Post*, 1 March 1991.
6. The chemical 'protection kits' alone, distributed to every resident (there were approximately five million residents) at a cost of 250 IS each, totalled 1.25 billion IS. Also cf. Note 4 above.
7. 'A year after the Gulf War', *Ma'ariv*, January 1992.
8. Levran, *SSM Memo*; Seth Carus, *Missiles in the M.E. – A New Threat to Stability* (Washington: The Washington Institute for Near East Policy), June 1988; *Ma'ariv Report*, ibid., p. 33; Major General Ze'ev Livneh, *Bamahane* (the IDF Weekly), 15 January 1992.
9. Y. Ben-Meir, 'The Israeli arena in the Gulf War' [Hebrew], in *The Gulf War*

– *Its Implications for Israel* (Jaffee Center for Strategic Studies, Tel Aviv University) 1991, p. 298 (hereafter *Gulf War – Implications*; interviews with Professor Kreitler and others in *Bamahane*, 13 March 1991; and interviews with Professors Elisha Efrat and Yehuda Gardos, *Bamahane*, 15 January 1992 ('An exercise in mass flight', p. 30).

10. Asher Arian, 'Security and political attitudes – impact of the Gulf War', in *Gulf War – Implications*, pp. 267, 269; Mina Tzemah, *Yediot Aharonot*, 25 January 1991.

11. Cf. Tzemah, *Yediot Aharonot*, ibid., and *Ma'ariv*, 1 February 1991 and 22 February 1991. In this connection it is worth mentioning that the war, although traumatic, apparently had little effect on Israeli public opinion, be it with respect to their perception of the threat, the use of military force, or other aspects, cf. G. Barzilai and E. Inbar, 'Do Wars Have an Impact?: Israeli Public Opinion after the Gulf War,' *Jerusalem Journal of International Relations*, No. 12, March 1992.

12. *Ma'ariv Report*, ibid., p. 41.

13. An interview with former IAF Commander General Ben-Nun in *Bitaon Heil Ha'avir* (hereafter the *IAF Journal*), October 1991. Several days before the outbreak of the war he made the following memorable remarks on Israeli television: 'A missile strike will destroy at most a room in an apartment or a structure.' Also cf. the comments by the head of aerial intelligence ('The missiles will cause only minimal damage . . .'), *Ma'ariv*, 8 September 1990.

14. Recall that Egypt's late President Sadat did not go to war against Israel in 1973 without first acquiring some Scud B missiles from the former USSR and some long-range combat aircraft from Libya and Saudi Arabia (Mirages and Lightnings, respectively).

15. Restricting their range to 150 km strips will deprive the missiles of their more important strategic uses. For Israel, however, due to the short distance from its borders to many of its population centres, even 150 km missiles have strategic connotations.

16. Levran, *SSM Memo*, 1988.

17. *Ha'aretz*, 21 April 1991; *Jane's Defence Weekly* (hereafter *JDW*), 17 April 1991, p. 677. 'The figure for Iraq's missile stockpile was subsequently amended to 61. It may have been as high as 150.'

18. Former Minister of Defence Moshe Arens: 'There are 20 to 30 missile launchers', *Ha'aretz*, 28 January 1991; General Schwarzkopf: 'All the stationary missile launchers have been destroyed, as well as 16 out of approximately 100 mobile missile launchers, according to American intelligence estimates', cited in *Yediot Aharonot*, 21 January 1991; former Deputy Chief of the General Staff E. Barak: 'In western Iraq there are 30 stationary missile launchers and 10–12 mobile missile launchers,' *Ha'aretz*, 4 February 1991; also cf. *Ma'ariv Report*, pp. 8, 13.

19. According to Professor Miller's study, published in the *New York Times* on 24 June 1992, and cited in *Ma'ariv*, 25 June 1992.

20. According to Miller's study; also cf. Arens' remarks to *Aviation Weekly*: 'To the best of my knowledge, not a single missile launcher was destroyed from the air', cited in *Ha'aretz*, 10 July 1991. Arens reported these words over the Israeli media on several other occasions.

21. Cf. Eliot Cohen, Director of the Air Survey, in 'The Air War in the Persian

Gulf', *Armed Forces Journal International* (*AFJI*), June 1991 (hereafter 'Air Survey').

22. Cited in *Ma'ariv*, 26 June 1991. 'We haven't been so successsful vs the SSMs.' This remark is also cited in Cheney's introduction to the Pentagon Report on the War, *Leadership and Planning Led to Persian Gulf Success*, 10 April 1992 (hereafter *Pentagon Report*).

23. Cited in *Ma'ariv*, 27 July 1992.

24. *Newsweek*, 17 June 1991; a similar story appeared in *AFJI*, July 1991.

25. *Ma'ariv*, 19 June 1992; *Tzevet* (the retired IDF officers' journal), No. 11, July 1991.

26. A distinction is made between a *sortie* (a successful flight, whether or not an aircraft releases ordnance) and a *strike* (the release of ordnance by a single aircraft on a given target). Usually strikes comprise 40–50 per cent of the total sorties in a war.

27. Cited in *Ma'ariv*, 29 January 1991; and especially in *Ha'aretz*, 28 January 1991 (there Schwarzkopf is cited as saying that he would not let the anti-missile effort change his priorities). There were even thoughts of transferring responsibility for fighting the missiles to the American command in Turkey (*Ha'aretz*, 15 February 1991).

28. *Tzevet*, ibid., July 1992; *Yediot Aharonot*, 19 June 1991, and *Ma'ariv Report*, 29 March 1991, p. 36. Also former Commander-in-Chief of the IDF, General Dan Shomron, was sure of this (cf. *Ma'ariv*, 28 February 1991) as was his deputy at the time, General Ehud Barak (cf. *Ha'aretz*, 4 February 1991) and the IAF Chief of Operations (cf. *Bamahane*, 6 March 1991). Dan Shomron also said that the US conferred continuously with Israel about crushing the missile threat (*Ha'aretz*, 3 February 1991).

29. Arens in an interview to the *AFJI*, as cited in *Ma'ariv*, 6 August 1991.

30. See the comment of the IDF AA forces commander in *Bamahane*, 11 February 1991, and the comment of the Commander of the IAF in the *IAF Journal*, June 1991. See also the author's contribution (A. Levran, 'Gulf War Lessons – An Israeli Perspective', unpublished paper written for CNSS, November 1991 in Patrick Garrity, *Why the Gulf War Still Matters: Foreign Perspectives on the War*, Center for National Strategic Studies, Los Alamos National Laboratories, July 1993, p. 55 – hereafter Los Alamos CNSS Report, No. 16).

31. R. Pedahtzur, *Ha'aretz*, 24 October 1991; *New York Times*, 31 October 1991.

32. *JDW*, 26 October 1991; *Bamahane*, 10 June 1992. Also cf. the remarks by the IDF AA forces commander that 'contrary to what has been publicised, some of the results [intercepting the missiles – A.L.] have been positive; in the war, the validity of SSM interception systems was borne out and the potential of the Patriot to carry out its mission was proven.' (*Bamahane*, 15 January 1992).

33. As Oscar Wilde has aptly said, 'What is a cynic? A man who knows the price of everything, and the value of nothing.'

34. Clinton remarks at the AIPAC conference, United States Information Agency, Tel Aviv, 29 April 1996.

35. A. Levite, 'Military lessons of the Gulf War', in *Gulf War – Implications*, p. 147.

2

The Rôle of Air Power
and Qualitative Weaponry
in the War

The Second Gulf War provided an impressive display of air power and advanced military technology. Despite certain evidence and opinions belittling this from the operational angle, it can be said that these two components were more central and even more decisive than others in the victory over Iraq.

LESSONS IN THE DOMAIN OF AIR POWER

A central strategic question which arises from the Second Gulf War is whether air power alone can win a war. This question has been of wide concern ever since the theory that air power alone can win a war was first espoused by the Italian, Douhet, and the American, Mitchell, in the wake of the First World War.[1] Subsequent views on this subject, based on the experience of several wars – the Second World War, the Korean War, the Vietnam War, as well as the Yom Kippur War – were not overly optimistic. Nevertheless, one could vehemently argue that the Second Gulf War was won by the Coalition's air force alone, for by 16 February 1991 Saddam Hussein had already expressed his willingness to withdraw from Kuwait. He took this stance again on 21 February 1991, when he sent his Foreign Minister Tariq Aziz to Moscow to negotiate withdrawal[2] almost a week before the ground attack was launched (24 February 1991).

Although air power alone did not win the wars that

preceded the Second Gulf War, its considerable contribution, even in those wars, is unquestionable. This was especially true when the belligerents' air forces were used properly – in other words against pin-point targets and objectives which, when adequately hit, promptly helped neutralise the enemy's war effort. Indeed, when air forces were not employed wisely – when they were used, for example, in carpet-bombing missions and for massively pounding enemy territory from the air, as in the Second World War and subsequent wars fought in the Far East, the results were not particularly encouraging.[3]

The Second Gulf War was neither the first, nor only, war to be won almost exclusively by air power.[4] Understandably, the Israel Air Force contributed decisively to the IDF's brilliant victory in the Six Day War (1967) by destroying dozens of enemy fighter planes on the ground during the first few hours of battle. For all its impressiveness, the victory in the air in the Second Gulf War was, by contrast, achieved under particularly favourable, even unique, circumstances which must not be overlooked.

The Coalition Air Force (CAF) undoubtedly had a clear quantitative and qualitative advantage over its adversary, the Iraqi Air Force. The Coalition possessed around 1,800 fighter aircraft, as well as hundreds of helicopters and transport and auxiliary planes, whereas Iraq had at its disposal about 700 fighter planes and several hundred helicopters and other aircraft.[5] Western planes and pilots and their auxiliary equipment were far superior in quality to those of Iraq. This was manifest in the small losses and depletion suffered by the CAF – a total of only 38 fighter planes and five helicopters.[6] Although this figure represents about two per cent of the Coalition's total aircraft and helicopters, in terms of the number of sorties executed in the war – approximately 118,000 – it is very low indeed (less than 0.4 per thousand, or one loss for every 2,700 flights). As far as we know, not a single plane was lost in air combat. By comparison, the Israel Air Force, the great victor in the 1967 war, lost about 12 per cent of its fighter aircraft in that war.

Even in regional terms the Iraqi Air Force was not a strong

adversary, and it was certainly no match for a superpower's air force. This became evident in the First Gulf War, when the Iraqi Air Force did not display much capability even against the weak Iranian air force with its poor air defences. Despite several impressive long-range air operations, the Iraqi Air Force was only successful in a small percentage of its bombing missions.[7] No wonder, then, that in the Second Gulf War, the Iraqi Air Force was not a serious opponent for the CAF for several reasons. First, in the few air battles that took place, 36 Iraqi planes and five Iraqi helicopters were downed, but not a single Coalition loss was sustained.[8] Second, after about ten days of battle the Iraqi Air Force decided to remain on the ground rather than contend with the Coalition in the air; moreover, 148 Iraqi planes defected to Iran, 115 of them being high quality combat planes.[9] The Coalition, therefore, rapidly achieved air supremacy due to Iraq's failure to make any response in the air and to the Coalition's suppression of Iraq's air defences – especially its SAM network.

The Coalition's air force also enjoyed the benefit of favourable initial battle conditions. Geographically and topographically, the Iraqi–Kuwaiti arena was extremely convenient: it consisted mostly of open desert terrain, providing an ideal setting for air operations. The Iraqis, unlike the Vietcong, for example, were not an evasive, hard-to-hit enemy. Moreover, Iraq, an economically more developed country than Vietnam or North Korea, had a wide range of vulnerable strategic assets that were particularly vulnerable to air attack. Moreover, the Coalition Air Force had almost no time limit or logistical constraints. Above all, the US did not have to worry about a potential superpower conflict. Being almost totally unhindered by such 'traditional' constraints, the CAF enjoyed great freedom of action in planning its operations, preparing for them, and implementing them at its own pace. This was manifest, *inter alia*, in the CAF being able to make repeated bombing raids on Iraqi targets, as it saw fit.[10]

The confluence of all these factors considerably eased the air campaign on Iraq and contributed to the victory in the air. Nevertheless, those who planned and implemented the air offensive deserve praise. This onslaught was successful in several respects. First, the air campaign in the Second Gulf War can generally be characterised as a 'surgical' battle against point targets. Second, the air command successfully launched and directed some 118,000 sorties of all types (combat, support, transportation, etc.)[11] in the course of 42 days of battle – some 2,800 flights of all sorts per day, but only around 1,300 combat strikes per day. This comes to slightly more than one flight per aircraft per day, excluding combat strikes. Although this rate of sorties and strikes is not overly impressive (in Israel's wars IAF aircraft averaged more than two, and sometimes even three, combat flights per day), it is not negligible, especially bearing in mind that several air forces and a large number and variety of planes were involved simultaneously in the theatre of operations. The great number of sorties and the high level of co-ordination were feasible due to the advanced operating systems (including computerisation) used by the theatre air command. The fairly intensive activity of CAF planes at night[12] also helped make such a large number of sorties possible. Night-time sorties doubled the overall flight volume and at the same time provided other considerable advantages, such as sustaining activity around the clock, allowing the enemy no respite, providing a measure of tactical surprise, and most important of all, minimising casualties.

Third, unlike in previous wars, the Coalition's aircraft used precision guided munitions (PGMs) and stand-off munitions quite intensively in the Second Gulf War and also made extensive use of electronic warfare systems. Although 'smart' munitions comprised only 6,250 tonnes of the 88,500 tonnes of air ordnance dropped in the war,[13] the air campaign was undoubtedly an impressive success due to this seven per cent of smart munitions. There is not much point in discussing the percentage of targets successfully hit by precision guided munitions (the Pentagon claims 90 per cent success, as opposed to 25 per cent for conventional bombs and munitions);[14] instead we prefer to dwell on the general impact of the munitions that were used and that led to victory in the war. PGMs, which were successful in hitting the hardened aircraft shelters on Iraq's airfields (an estimated 375 out of approximately 600 such pens were hit),[15] as well as the airfields themselves,[16] clearly showed the Iraqis their vulnerability and helplessness, forcing them to give up the battle in the air and run their aircraft out to Iran. PGMs and stand-off munitions alone, coupled with massive electronic warfare, hit about half of Iraq's SAM launchers and neutralised the others, bringing down Iraq's air defences in a few days. This put Iraq's infrastructure and military forces at the mercy of the Coalition's aircraft and also enabled the 82,000 tonnes of conventional ('dumb') bombs to have a greater effect than in previous wars.[17]

Fourth, whereas bombing Iraq's strategic objectives such as command and control centres, civilian infrastructure (electricity plants, oil depots and lines, bridges, and so forth), and facilities for producing weapons of mass destruction (research and development centres, stockpiles, and so forth) was only partially successful (as became evident later on), bombing its military forces and deployed weapons systems, especially the Republican Guard in northern Kuwait and southern Iraq, had a greater impact and proved more successful. According to Pentagon sources, the aerial attack on that region destroyed approximately 1,700 tanks and 1,400 guns, whereas (according to the same sources) 1,300 tanks and 740 guns were destroyed both from the air and the ground in the 100-hour ground offensive.[18] Perhaps the Americans had hoped to destroy more in their aerial attacks. (As it is, these figures for quantities destroyed might be an exaggeration.)[19] Nevertheless, after 40 days and nights of repeated bombing, hitting armaments and supply lines and cutting off Iraqi forces from the rear, these forces were in no condition to put up a serious fight; incessant air attacks had shattered their will to fight. This was evident primarily in the case of the land battle. The devastating effect of the aerial attacks on Iraqi forces and morale could be seen in the last days of the war in the televised pictures of thousands of miserable Iraqi soldiers with no fighting spirit surrendering *en masse*.

The combination of PGMs, stand-off munitions, and electronic warfare support measures (ESM) played a major rôle in keeping Coalition casualties to a minimum.[20] It is clear that the war would have been assessed quite differently had the casualty rate been high – a much-dreaded risk. Moreover, since the 'simple' Iraqi anti-aircraft weapons caused the Coalition losses in the first days of the war, the Coalition had to fly its planes at, and attack from, altitudes of 12,000 to 18,000 feet and only PGMs and aerial stand-off munitions could compensate for the loss of accuracy in bombing from such a high altitude. These weapons, which could be operated equally well from advanced or outdated aircraft, made feasible both night-time attacks and strikes on highly fortified Iraqi targets. They thus contributed to reducing casualties and to tactically surprising the enemy.

Despite the obvious qualitative advantages enjoyed by the CAF, it was becoming increasingly evident that the aerial campaign was not entirely a success story from the operational point of view. As we shall see, this campaign had substantial failings both in intelligence (to be discussed in the next chapter) and in actual operations.

In the operational sphere, it appears that many of the targets attacked were not properly hit. Since Coalition aircraft had sufficient time and adequate munitions, it seems that their lack of success may have arisen from a lack of the requisite expertise in aerial operations, primarily in battle damage assessment capability (BDA). A larger measure of such expertise could have compensated for insufficiently precise or destructive aerial strikes. It is hard to understand how large and easily-hit targets such as oil refineries were not hit properly. Two months after the war the Iraqis boasted that the refineries were back in operation;[21] yet we have no solid information that the CAF deliberately refrained from inflicting heavy damage on them. Similarly, in mid-July 1992, it was already reported that, of the 130 Iraqi bridges that had been attacked, 120 had already been rebuilt. The same was true of other targets, such as the electrical network, which was rapidly (in terms of several months) restored. In fact, in January 1993 (two years after Desert Storm), the Americans again attacked a nuclear

installation in Za'afraniya, outside Baghdad, with 45 (!) Tomahawk cruise missiles. This installation had been bombed in the
war, but appears to have survived and continued functioning.
(Perhaps this is also indicative of Iraq's rapid reconstruction
capability,[22] although the scope and quality of such reconstruction is uncertain.)

The failure of the aerial campaign was most notable in the
fight against Iraq's SSMs. As we have mentioned, the US
air force did not prepare properly for this task. We know
that, in the course of the war, a variety of methods of aerial
attack were employed and that ground forces were involved.
If the Americans had employed an adequate approach and
a suitable operational doctrine for combating mobile SSMs,
they would have succeeded even with the 1,500 or so strikes
which they devoted to this task (assuming that only about
half of the total of 3,000 sorties in western Iraq was aimed at
SSM targets, and that the other half was aimed at suspicious
sites, bridges, water carriers, moving vehicles, and so forth).
It is clear that the Coalition aircraft in western Iraq also
suffered from a lack of tactical intelligence, even though
Joint Surveillance Target and Attack Radar System (JSTARS)
radar planes were allocated to the task of locating the SSMs,
and despite the fact that the F-15Es (Eagles) and other
advanced aircraft operating in the area had their own tools for
intelligence gathering. The problem, however, was primarily
one of a faulty approach and insufficient combat expertise.
For example, the CAF attacked fixed-site missile launchers
with great verve, although the mobile missile launchers were
actually the principal challenge.[23]

Interestingly, climatic conditions also made the work of the
CAF more difficult. From time to time heavy cloud cover
disrupted air operations and prevented the infra-red sensors
installed in many of the planes and weapons systems from
functioning properly.[24] Notwithstanding impressive technological developments, bad weather can still be a significant
hindrance to air operations. This can be critical at certain
stages of combat when air power is needed above all else.
In other words, in planning combat operations, one cannot

and should not rely on one's air force alone. This is particularly true for Israel, which counts so much on its air power because of its inherent quantitative inferiority.

What do we learn from all this? To begin with, this analysis stresses well-known truths. First and foremost, even though an air campaign can pave the way for victory, it is not sufficient; other military means are required, certainly including a ground offensive. In the Second Gulf War, even after six weeks of bombing from the air, a land manoeuvre was still necessary in order to physically bring the war to a close and to achieve its main objectives, namely, to drive the Iraqis out of Kuwait and to restore the latter's government. Had the US accepted Saddam Hussein's offers for cessation of the war of 16 February and 21 February 1991, which incidentally were conditional, this would have been interpreted as an Iraqi victory.[25] As it was, within Iraq the outcome of the war was (falsely) presented as an Iraqi victory; selling such a claim would have been even easier if there had not been a ground offensive which out-flanked the Iraqi army, throwing it off balance, and forcing it out of Kuwait. The Iraqis would also have interpreted an absence of a land offensive as indicating that the Coalition, and in particular the Americans, were afraid to confront Iraq's army face to face, as Saddam had indeed maintained during the war.[26] In particular, without the land battle, large segments of the Republican Guard, the mainstay of Iraq's army, would have come through unscathed. Thus, the ground offensive was necessary to achieve Iraq's unconditional surrender. Apparently it was also necessary for US–Arab relations after the war, to provide a tangible illustration of American military might, to strengthen Arab bonds to the US, and to enhance their willingness to co-operate.

The Second Gulf War was not exceptional in requiring a ground campaign in order to bring the war to a close. In the First Gulf War Iraq had been freely attacking Iranian forces and infrastructure from the air for eight years, but it was unable to terminate the war until its army began a ground offensive (on 18 April 1988), and won back all the territory it had lost to Iran. The same is true of the Six Day War. In spite of the brilliant air victory of the first few hours, Israel still had to conquer the Sinai Peninsula, the Golan Heights and other areas, with ground troops.

A double lesson can be learned from this. Air power alone is apparently not sufficient to bring a war to a decisive end but it is invaluable for victory and survival. To win a war one must have a strong air force that can rapidly achieve air supremacy, accomplish its objectives – air superiority, interdiction, attacking strategic targets, and so forth – and provide air cover and support for ground forces. This, however, does not imply that a nation with a formidable air force will necessarily win any conflict, under any circumstances.

Another important lesson is that even an air campaign which is not a complete operational success can be a success from the strategic point of view. We have observed the shortcomings of the CAF air offensive, yet it is clear beyond a doubt that Iraq was defeated in the Second Gulf War. Despite its rhetoric, by accepting all the UN resolutions Iraq acknowledged its defeat. Saddam Hussein was forced to accept humiliating limitations on his country's sovereignty such as a Kurd enclave placed under UN jurisdiction and many intrusive supervisory operations by UN teams. Every time Iraq tries to revolt against these strict limitations and appears to be heading for a confrontation, in the end it backs down and gives in to the UN and, essentially, to the US. Since late August 1992, Iraq has been forbidden from flying its aircraft south of the 32nd parallel and Saddam has had to comply, notwithstanding his protests. Saddam's compliance with these restrictions undoubtedly stems from the recognition that Iraq is weak, especially in terms of air power. Even though the only danger threatening Iraq after the war was a US attack from the air on a far smaller scale than during the war, nevertheless Saddam was careful not to become embroiled in a serious confrontation with the US again.

Thus an air battle, even if only partially successful, can still manifest the vulnerability of the side attacked and the uselessness of resorting to war. It suffices for air power to throw the adversary off balance in order to help bring about a decisive victory. The fact that every strategic resource in Iraq, including its armed forces, was at the mercy of the Coalition's air power sufficed to make Saddam realise that he had been defeated. Disclosure of what remained in Iraq after the war, however, took the edge off this defeat, even though much had supposedly been destroyed or damaged. Moreover, the partial air success may have indicated to Saddam that the American threat is not so dreadful and that he is not taking too great a risk in delaying implementation of UN resolutions and occasionally challenging Washington's determination.

As far as Israel is concerned, the clearly acknowledged implications are that Israel should continue giving high priority to the IDF's air force and sophisticated weaponry, while also stressing the importance of IAF's offensive missions against vital strategic enemy objectives, as was done in the Yom Kippur War (1973) against Syria. The last Gulf War illustrated the importance of strategic air strikes. It also illustrated the need to ensure that air attacks on strategic enemy objectives are as successful as possible by planning them adequately and by providing the appropriate munitions and offensive methods. Likewise, Israel can only prove itself victorious if its air supremacy is properly felt and extensively demonstrated.

QUALITATIVE WEAPONRY AND MUNITIONS

The Second Gulf War provided an impressive display of advanced Western military technology. In no previous war had so many smart munitions or advanced weapons systems been used. There are also firm grounds for maintaining that this high quality technology was decisive in winning the war.

It is not our intention here to analyse or describe the performance of each of these weapons, munitions, and support systems in the Second Gulf War; but we shall make several general observations about their use. Our concern is primarily with the macro-strategic aspects of employing these weapons, and not with the tactical-professional aspects. In addition, quite a few details pertaining to the operation of smart weapons in this war are still classified or have been publicised in distorted form. After all, the war served as a field for trial runs with these weapons and munitions.

One observation worth noting is the rise in the relative weight of fire power in the art of warfare, although the other pillar of warfare – manoeuvrability or troop movement – remains as vital as ever in conventional warfare. This is due to more extensive use of PGMs and smart weapons. Whereas, in the past, targets could be destroyed by statistical weapons (such as artillery), with all their well-known shortcomings, or by ground force manoeuvres, today this can be done equally well, if not better, from afar and by PGMs. This apparently makes fire power relatively more important in comparison to manoeuvrability in a conventional war, and particularly in deciding its outcome. Thus, in the Second Gulf War, from the onset of battle operations, a combination of fire power and electronic warfare became essentially the dominant and decisive factor. The question still remains as to whether the Second Gulf War can serve as a model for wars between local, 'traditional' adversaries in the Middle East. Be that as it may, more Middle Eastern countries today are trying to acquire PGMs and smart weapons, and are thus underscoring the increased importance of fire power in war.

A second observation relates to the constant dichotomy between quantity and quality with respect to weapons systems. PGMs and smart weapons (in addition to air power) symbolise, above all, the core of military quality. Nevertheless, it should be noted that the Coalition, especially the US, did not rely exclusively on quality, but also saw to it that large quantities of manpower, arms and munitions were amassed before the war.[27] This was not only due to uncertainty regarding the performance of the new qualitative weaponry in the war. The Second Gulf War, like other major wars in the Middle East, such as the First Gulf War and the Yom Kippur War, illustrated (once more) that quantity is an extremely important factor in warfare. On the other hand, it is true that sophisticated weapons systems and munitions can serve as force multipliers, compensating for relative numerical inferiority of forces or other military handicaps. However, qualitative weaponry alone cannot tip the balance of forces between adversaries simply by the stroke of a wand. In order to obtain the maximum benefit from qualitative weapons systems one also needs higher quality manpower to operate the weapons. Qualitative weapons in the hands of mediocre operators is no panacea for military problems. In this respect the IDF has a clear advantage over its adversaries, due to its better integration of high quality manpower and sophisticated weaponry. Indeed, one of the lessons the Arabs have learned from the war is that they must strengthen themselves in terms of qualitative weapons and munitions; but without also having high quality operators they will only derive partial benefit from such weapon enhancement.

One should bear in mind that smart weapons comprised only seven per cent of the total ordnance dropped on the Iraqis. It is interesting to speculate whether this was because they were 90 per cent successful in hitting the target,[28] according to Pentagon claims, or because they were so expensive.[29] True, smart weapons are costly (and this is generally what hinders greater reliance on them); yet ordinary munitions are not cheap either, if one considers the real inclusive cost of dropping such ordnance, which apparently only scored successful hits 25 per cent of the time. If one calculates the real cost, taking into account the necessary ancillary expenses involved in using regular munitions, such as requiring more aircraft for bombing missions (in addition to attack aircraft, one also needs planes for air cover and interception, refuelling, electronic warfare, reconnaissance, and so forth), as well as the larger quantities of ordnance that must be dropped, then it comes as no surprise that PGMs are not overly expensive. Due to the specific circumstances of the Second Gulf War, the rate of target destruction was higher with smart weapons than with conventional ones; and this, after all, is the critical factor in any war and a touchstone for its outcome.

The quantity of PGMs and stand-off munitions launched in the war, in view of their high precision, was far from negligible.

The US fired some 300 Tomahawk cruise missiles from its navy's ships and submarines (out of a total of about 540 such missiles which the US brought to the Gulf), approximately 2,900 Hellfire air-to-surface missiles (fired from Apache helicopters), several tens of thousands of Maverick air-to-surface missiles, some 8,000 laser-guided bombs, about 1,000 HARM missiles (designed to detect and destroy radar sites by homing-in on their emissions), dozens of SLAM cruise missiles from the fleet's aircraft, and more.[30]

Another aspect of advanced weapons and munitions, as manifest in the war, made it possible to apply Liddel Hart's time-honoured and important doctrine of *indirect approach*, although in a somewhat different manner, namely by using the factor of fire power and not troop manoeuvre. Instead of trying to contend head-on with well-defended (and, therefore, dangerous) targets, aircraft could approach and attack indirectly, using smart weapons and stand-off munitions. In other words, PGMs offer a new means of destruction from a distance. Thus, Liddel Hart's theory of indirect approach can now be implemented with fire power rather than manoeuvres.[31] Moreover, the most dangerous air defences for the CAF, including SAM batteries, were attacked by stand-off means such as HARM air-to-surface missiles in conjunction with massive use of electronic weapons. Precision-guided missiles also facilitated increased precision attacks from higher altitudes.

The indirect attack and evasive capabilities of the Coalition's aircraft were primarily manifest by the Stealth F-117A jet. Even though, according to reports, the two Stealth squadrons (54 jets)[32] comprised only 2.5 per cent of the air force, they carried out 31 per cent of the attacks made on Iraqi targets in the first day of combat. The second stage of the air campaign included vital objectives of three types: those related to Iraq's offensive capability; targets of strategic and political importance (which were chosen to undermine Iraq's infrastructure and the régime itself); and targets related to production capability and use of non-conventional arms. These objectives were in addition to the classic mission of any air force – achieving air superiority. Since almost all of these targets were well fortified, they were attacked primarily by Stealth aircraft. These aircraft could penetrate Iraqi air defences without having to be escorted by other aircraft with electronic weapons systems or by cover aircraft and interceptors, and even without having to suppress air defences first.

There is an interesting report concerning eight Stealth aircraft successfully mounting an attack on the nuclear centre in Tuwaitha (south-east of Baghdad), after some 75 conventional planes, mostly F-16s, had failed in their attempts to attack it due to SAM launchings and smoke screens. The Stealth bombers, by contrast, launched 16 smart missiles or bombs which hit 16 secondary targets at the nuclear complex and systematically destroyed it.[33] The combination of the F-117, laser bombs (GBU-24), and electro-optical bombs (GBU-15) succeeded in destroying around 95 per cent of the principal targets in Baghdad with minimal damage to the surrounding area.[34] Minimising surrounding damage, especially to civilians, is especially important in wars that are closely followed by television cameras[35] and is important in its own right. Precision bombing was also used against the air force headquarters and air defences in Baghdad. Not a single Stealth jet was downed in this war.

Advanced technology also made it possible to achieve its old objective of significant night-time fighting capability. Indeed, most of the principal hardware used in the Gulf could be used at night, especially the F-117A jets,[36] the Apache helicopters, and the Abrams tanks, as well as the weapons installed in them or the munitions operated independently from a distance, such as cruise and other missiles (Tomahawks, SLAMs, and so forth). It was reported that the Apache helicopters began the war by destroying some of Iraq's air detection radar equipment in the dark, thus opening an air corridor through which hundreds of aircraft could safely attack their targets. These helicopters also played an important part in the ground battle, primarily against the Republican Guard, especially at night. About 275 Apache helicopters were used, firing some 2,875 Hellfire missiles.[37] Night-time fighting capability was extremely important in reducing casualties, in surprising the enemy, and in maintaining the momentum of attack around the clock (to the extent that some observers termed this a 24-hour war); all this was apart from its contribution in enabling attacks on well-defended objectives. Night-time fighting capability coupled with smart electronic warfare thus contributed to physically and emotionally debilitating the Iraqi army until it collapsed, both in Kuwait and in southern Iraq.

Another facet of the use of smart weapons in the Second Gulf War concerns the extent to which such weapons will be used in the future and the place of old weapons systems in combat today. Here, too, the Second Gulf War teaches us an ancient truth: the process is primarily evolutionary, not revolutionary. To begin with, old weapons were used in the Second Gulf War alongside new ones and even in conjunction with them; and, interestingly, the old weapons proved successful. After the Yom Kippur War some individuals maintained that the advent of the missile heralded the end of the era of the airplane; yet in the Second Gulf War we witnessed successful action by all sorts of fixed-wing aircraft, including such obsolete models as the A-7, A-10, F-111, B-52, and A-6, as well as the newer generation of aircraft such as the F-15 (including the F-15E), F-16, F-18, F-117A, AH-64 helicopters (Apaches), and others. Moreover, precision and stand-off munitions, such as SLAM missiles, installed in the navy's older aircraft – such as the A-6E – enhanced both the efficacy and the survivability of these aircraft. The war also illustrated (once more) that older, simple weapons, such as the Iraqi anti-aircraft guns, were a greater threat to Coalition aircraft than the more advanced SAMs.

Even though advanced electronic warfare and smart weapons (such as the Stealth aircraft, the Apache helicopters, and PGMs) might revolutionise combat on the battlefield of the future, development of the art of warfare, like that of weapons, proceeds according to a dialectic process. Whenever a new weapon appears in the arena, a new countermeasure is developed, and so on. Thus, at best, one can speak of a revolution in weaponry in relative, temporal terms. The same holds for the traditional dichotomy between tanks and anti-tank weapons. The latter succeeded in the Yom Kippur War, and some people even predicted the demise of the tank on the battlefield of the future. However, in 1991, we observed the clear superiority of the American Abrams tanks and the British Challengers (impenetrable from the front even by advanced anti-tank missiles, and in the future they will be impenetrable from other sides too).[38] Likewise, American aircraft had no difficulty defeating Iraqi SAMs. The Israel Air Force first demonstrated that this was feasible in 1982 against Syrian SAMs deployed on the Lebanese–Syrian border. The same will surely prove to be the case in meeting the challenge of SSMs by means of anti-missiles or other appropriate alternatives.

WHAT WON THE WAR?

We have no intention of pin-pointing the specific reasons for the Coalition's victory here. There was undoubtedly more than one reason, but the most prominent was that the balance of power and military capabilities was not in Iraq's favour from the outset. Her unwise policies only added to her inevitable defeat. We intend to focus here more on the main types of weapons which led to victory.

In this regard, it is worth citing Israel Air Force Commander, Major General Herzl Bodinger, who stated that it was not PGMs that determined the outcome of the Gulf War, but rather the sheer might and massive force at the disposal of the US.[39] Regarding the use of PGMs in the Second Gulf War, 'many legends,' he said, 'have been told about this weaponry, and the aura surrounding it far exceeds its true dimensions.'[40] The then Deputy Chief of the General Staff, Ehud Barak, also spoke in a similar vein: 'The war displayed the current potential of smart weapons, more than it realised this potential.'[41] While Bodinger's remarks might be attributed to a fear that limited resources will be channelled towards PGMs at the expense of the air force and its aircraft, the remarks of the Chief of the General Staff are based on an overall view.

Perhaps the success of the advanced weaponry and PGMs has been portrayed in somewhat exaggerated terms. The Americans themselves are aware of this and are currently working on improvements even in such modern weapons systems as the F-117, the Apache, the Patriot, and others. It is also true that the US, a superpower, had at her disposal a far more massive force than Iraq, whose victory over Iran in the First Gulf War had caused it to lose all sense of proportion.

In our opinion, each of these factors – massive force and PGMs – and especially their conjunction in the Second Gulf War, proved to Saddam Hussein the limitations of his military strength. It is interesting that, in a speech a year after the war, even Saddam saw fit to admit that he had been beaten in terms of technology and materiel, although not in terms of morale.[42] Although it is hard to prove, each of these factors alone probably would not have been sufficient to terminate the war, certainly not with such speed and low Coalition casualty figures. Hence, we may conclude that the combination of massive air and military power with point precision capabilities made such a clear-cut, swift victory possible and rendered the continuation of the war pointless. Aside from the dramatic impression that advanced technology might have on a distressed opponent, psychology in war does count.

Smart weapons and stand-off munitions, whose combatworthiness was demonstrated again in the Second Gulf War (following the 1982 Lebanese War) proved the validity of the doctrine held by the IDF, which had adopted such weapons a decade earlier, and also proved the need to continue to expand efforts in this direction. The IDF has always been distinguished from its adversaries by its technological superiority and qualitative weapons (and its excellent and highly motivated manpower). The Second Gulf War should reinforce the trend in this direction. It has also added substantially to our knowledge of various weapons based on combat experience.

NOTES

1. Douhet's book, *Air Supremacy* (in Italian) was written in 1921, and Mitchell's *Winged Defense* in 1925. Another important study is M. E. Smith, 'The Strategic Bombing Debate in WW II and Vietnam', *Journal of Contemporary History*, 12 (1977).
2. *Ha'aretz*, 17 February 1991; *Ma'ariv*, February 17 and 22 1991.
3. A. Levran, 'Twelve years after the Yom Kippur War – Strategic Aerial Bombing of Syria', *Ha'aretz*, 23 September 1985.
4. As former Minister of Defence Moshe Arens maintains in an interview in *Ha-Lohem* (the IDF invalids' journal), April 1991, p. 24.
5. Brigadier General Ben-Eliyahu (IAF Deputy Commander), *Ma'arakhot* (the IDF's Bimonthly) No. 321, May–June 1991; *Aviation Week*, 11 March 1991; and Air Marshal R. Mason, 'The Air War in the Gulf', *Survival*, May–June 1991.
6. *JDW*, 6 April 1991; *Aviation Week*, ibid.; and 'Pentagon Report'.
7. Cf. Mason's article in *Survival*; also A. Levran, 'Strategic Air Attacks in the Gulf War', in *The Middle East Military Balance 1987–1988* (Boulder: Westview Press, 1988).
8. *JDW*, 6 April 1991; *Aviation Week*, 11 March 1991; and 'Pentagon Report', ibid., April 1992.
9. The Iraqi Foreign Minister stated that 148 aircraft were flown to Iran, including 115 combat planes, among which were 75 Sukhoi aircraft, 24 Mirage HF1s, 16 Migs, etc. Cf. *Ma'ariv*, 14 April 1991. American intelligence estimated that only 137 Iraqi aircraft were run to Iran, *JDW*, 6 and 27 April 1991.
10. Cf. General Schwarzkopf's remarks, cited in *Ma'ariv*, 31 January 1991.
11. As mentioned, it is generally estimated that actual combat strikes comprise only about 45 per cent of the total sorties made.
12. *JDW*, 6 April 1991; *Israel Air Force Journal*, April 1991; 'Air Survey', ibid.
13. *Washington Post*, 16 March 1991; A. Cordesman, 'Rushing to Judgment', *AFJI*, June 1991.
14. Comment by the American Air Force Commander in *Defense and Diplomacy*, July–August 1991, pp. 57–60; also Cordesman, ibid.
15. Brigadier General Ben-Eliyahu, in the *IAF Journal*, April 1991, mentions that 300 out of more than 500 aircraft shelters were hit. The 'Air Survey' (ibid.), however, gives the figures cited above.
16. General Schwarzkopf: 'We attacked 38 airfields, and at some of them we struck at least four times', cited in *Ma'ariv*, 31 January 1991.
17. Cf. Cordesman, ibid.
18. *JDW*, 6 April 1991; *Time*, 11 April 1991, p. 38.
19. According to the 'Air Survey,' ibid., air power destroyed only one quarter of the armour of the Republican Guard before the ground war began and more than half of the armour in front line units.
20. The US had 79 fatalities (29 of them from the missile in Daharan), and total Coalition fatalities came to 126.
21. *Ma'ariv*, 19 and 30 April 1991; on 29 January 1991, *Ha'aretz* had already reported *moderate damage to three refineries and eight to nine petrochemical factories*.

22. Instructive testimony was given by one of the UN inspectors, David Kay, who noted that Iraq's reconstruction of its electrical network is an indication of the level of engineering and administrative expertise in Iraq (*Ma'ariv*, 3 August 1992). The Voice of Israel reported on Iraq's reconstruction of her bridges (15 July 1992), basing its report on a *New York Times* article from the previous day. Similarly, *Newsweek* (12 July 1992) reported that, according to American satellite photographs, the Iraqis are rebuilding the chemical and biological factories and installations damaged in the bombing. Also cf. *Ma'ariv*, 13 July 1992; *Bamahane*, 19 June 1991; by contrast, General Colin Powell, Chairman of the Joint Chiefs of Staff, boasted that 'in the war we took care of Baghdad's electrical system', (cited in *Ha'aretz*, 24 January 1991). In the 'Air Survey', ibid., E. Cohen writes that the Coalition planners 'intended to wreak severe but reversible damage to the electrical facilities, oil refineries, etc., but in actuality they could not adhere to their initial plans.' None the less, the Iraqis managed to restore most of their power system within a year of the war's end.

23. *Ha'aretz*, 15 February 1991.

24. On poor atmospheric conditions disrupting the functioning of laser bombs, cf. *Defense and Diplomacy*, ibid.; also *JDW*, 6 April 1991; *Ha'aretz*, 24 January 1991.

25. On those two occasions, and especially the first, Saddam agreed to retreat and is cited as saying that otherwise Iraq would face 'destruction and darkness'; however he added a number of arrogant conditions, such as demanding that Iraq be given war reparations and that her debts be forgiven. Cf. *Ha'aretz* and *Ma'ariv*, 17 February 1991.

26. In his speech of 21 February 1991, Saddam boasted of being 'sure America is afraid of a ground confrontation with us', *Ma'ariv*, 22 February 1991.

27. On the large quantities and varieties of weapons and manpower brought to the Gulf, see 'Air Survey', ibid.

28. *JDW*, 6 April 1991.

29. Various figures have been cited with respect to cost. In any event 'smart' weapons are quite expensive. Note the figures in *JDW* (6 April 1991): every precision bomb costs $100,000–130,000; a Tomahawk missile, ten times as much; an air-to-surface missile around $20,000; and a Patriot missile some $750,000. According to *Defense and Diplomacy*, July–August 1991. (Note 33) pp. 57–60, the SLAM (Stand-Off Land Attack Missile, operated by the Navy) costs approximately $800,000.

30. *JDW*, 25 April and 2 May 1992; also *Defense and Diplomacy*, ibid., and *Aviation Week*, 3 May 1991.

31. Cf. A. Levran, 'Los Alamos CNSS Report', ibid., No. 16, p. 64.

32. *JDW*, 25 April 1991.

33. *JDW*, 6 October 1991

34. *Defense and Diplomacy*, ibid.

35. This was underscored in the war when the Al-Firdos bunker was mistakenly attacked on 13 February 1991 causing hundreds of civilian casualties.

36. For example, *JDW*, 25 April 1991, notes that every Stealth bomber flew two missions per night. On the night-time onslaught, cf. the 'Air Survey', ibid.

37. *Time*, 11 March 1991; *JDW*, 2 May 1991, cites a report of the General

Accountant's Office (GAO), the congressional comptroller, based on a US Army report on Apache performance in the war, noting that the Apache was used for armed air reconnaissance more than its other primary function – as an anti-tank weapon – due to its sophisticated night vision. It also noted that the Apache had a 93 per cent success record, and that certain functional problems had been discovered in the helicopter and were being rectified.

38. Cf. the interview with Major General (Res.) Tal, *Ma'ariv*, 4 April 1991.
39. *IAF Journal*, February 1992.
40. *Ma'ariv*, 15 June 1992.
41. *Yediot Aharonot*, 29 September 1991.
42. Cited in the *Jerusalem Post*, 19 January 1992.

3

Functioning of US Intelligence in the Crisis and the War

There is considerable evidence that, after the war, attempts at gathering intelligence about Iraq were not entirely successful. Even though Coalition intelligence about Iraq was quite substantial, it was seriously lacking both in the domain of strategic and operational intelligence expertise. While a lack of intelligence information on the strategic level was a problem common to all the intelligence organisations opposing Iraq – US, European, Arab, and Israeli – on the operational level the burden of these failings fell entirely on the shoulders of Western intelligence organisations, especially the US. Although up-to-date, precise, extensive, and relevant information is essential for winning a war, and a lack of such intelligence is likely to lead to defeat, the overwhelming operational-technological superiority of the Coalition, and its vast advantage in the total balance of forces, were sufficient for victory, despite inadequate intelligence information.

INTELLIGENCE SHORTCOMINGS ON THE STRATEGIC LEVEL

On the strategic level, three serious intelligence failures stand out: being strategically surprised by the outbreak of the Kuwait crisis; seriously overestimating the real strength of Iraq's armed forces; and grossly underestimating her ambitious nuclear programme.[1]

The Kuwait crisis, sparked by Iraq's invasion of her smaller neighbour, was one more surprise in a long list of strategic surprises in modern history. The crisis came as a shock to everyone – the invasion victims themselves, namely the Kuwaitis, their Arab neighbours, including Saudi Arabia and Egypt (President Mubarak later lamented, 'Saddam lied to me when he gave me his word that he would not invade Kuwait'),[2] and the United States, despite all its sophisticated intelligence gathering systems such as satellites and AWACS. Even Israel, with its greater sensitivity to Saddam Hussein's threats, was none the less taken by surprise.[3]

The disquieting question is why such surprises keep recurring. An important general reason for the failure of early warning, and one which lay behind the strategic surprise in the Kuwait crisis, involves dichotomy between 'facts' and 'intentions'. As in other cases of surprise, the facts of an imminent military danger were actually evident yet a critical failure occurred in misreading the aggressor's intentions. In strategic confrontations, focusing too narrowly on 'intentions' instead of hard 'facts' is almost always the undoing of the party surprised. In late May 1990, at the Arab summit in Baghdad, Saddam Hussein had expressed his outrage over 'the economic war that was being fought against Iraq by several of the Gulf states' by flooding the world market with petroleum, lowering prices, and cutting into Iraqi revenues. On 17 July 1990, Saddam explicitly and pointedly accused Kuwait of being the country behind the 'economic war' and of 'stabbing Iraq in the back'. A week later, by 24 July 1990 (nine days before the invasion), two Iraqi armoured divisions were already lined up on the Kuwaiti border.[4]

Focusing on ominous 'facts', such as massive concentration of troops in the field and near the victim's border, is not sufficient, apparently, to trigger a strategic alarm; the victims of the surprise also have to believe that the aggressor indeed intends to carry out his plans and instruct his troops to march. This plunges us into a complex but well-known problem – that of reading an opponent's intentions correctly. In almost all the cases of strategic surprise, the difficulty lay in misreading the aggressor's intentions and failing to anticipate his decision to carry them out, especially when the aggressor's intentions involved a radical departure from his former, long-established and familiar policies and behaviour.

An opponent's strategic intentions are difficult to read for the following reasons:

- Decisions on radical policy changes are taken at the highest level and in the smallest circles of government, often by a single person, and do not leak out. This is especially true in authoritarian régimes. Collecting information from the narrow pinnacle of the adversary's pyramid of authority was and always will be more difficult than collecting information from the broad base; intelligence penetration at such a high level, which constitutes a narrow, close circle, is not an easy task.

- Another difficulty in locating radical policy changes has to do with the time factor. Generally, the time that elapses between a decision to make a dramatic change in policy, such as going to war, and the implementation of such a decision is too short for opposing intelligence organisations to learn of the decision and act upon it.

- Facts in the field, such as the massing of troops and other military preparations which might relate to a drastic change in enemy policy, can be interpreted in more than one way and can be viewed in different contexts. For example, Israeli intelligence interpreted the massing of Syrian troops on the Golan Heights on the eve of the Yom Kippur War (in September 1973) as being related to the air clash in which 13 of their planes were downed by the IAF on 13 September of that year.

- 'Facts' are generally and naturally accompanied by 'background noise' – other facts that obscure the truly significant ones. Only 'in hindsight' (as Roberta Wohlstetter puts it) can one distinguish the genuine facts from the misleading or unimportant ones, or as she says, the 'signals from the noise'.

- Misreadings of enemy intentions also stem from the victim's state of mind and from self-deception. This is especially true when the victim becomes locked into a rigid doctrinal framework. This happened to Stalin, for example, before Germany's invasion of the USSR (Operation Barbarossa) in the Second World War, and to Israel on the eve of the Yom Kippur War. In both these instances and others a reasonable explanation could be offered for the ominous actions of the other side.

Most of these factors lay behind the misreading of Saddam Hussein's intentions, even after the extremely advanced deployment of Iraqi armoured divisions became known. At the time, the general feeling, especially in the US, was that 'Saddam will not dare to attack and break the rules of the "new world order"'; that 'Saddam is just lying or trying to put on pressure' (since 'Iraq sacrificed enough blood, sweat and tears in the First Gulf War and will not rush into a new adventure'); and that 'at most, he will limit himself to capturing a few small bits of Kuwait,'[5] (such as the northern oil fields of Rumaylah and the Bubiyan and Warba Islands). The US was clearly still in a state of euphoria from the victory in the global confrontation between the West and the Soviet bloc.

Moreover, for years, at least since mid-1982 (when Iraq withdrew her forces from Iranian soil in the First Gulf War and sought to bring that war to a close), the US had definitely misread Saddam. The instances of ill-advised US aid to Iraq during that war are too numerous to mention. It is therefore no surprise that one week before the invasion, on 25 July 1990, the US Ambassador to Baghdad told Saddam that the Administration considered him a 'moderate and peace-loving leader', and, more importantly, that the Administration had 'no intention of interfering in border disputes between Iraq and Kuwait' (or, for that matter, between any two Arab states).[6] This was nothing more than an expression of the distorted and long-standing fixation in the Bush Administration's way of thinking about Saddam Hussein, perceiving him as a moderate ruler, well-suited to arrest the spread of Khomeinism in the region. The US persisted in its approach notwithstanding the many cautionary voices raised in Israel and in Congress, which were ignored by the Administration. This perception not only hindered American ability to read Saddam's intentions correctly, but encouraged Saddam to go ahead with his violation of Kuwait. As far as we are concerned, the reason the US did not direct sufficient intelligence efforts towards Iraq[7] was due to their mistaken reading of the Iraqi ruler and his régime.

Unfortunately, there is no panacea for errors in assessment. 'Misjudgements' are actually one of the harsh facts of strategy and pose a constant threat to small states struggling for survival, especially states with neighbours still not ready to accept their sovereign existence. Of course, deeper intelligence penetration into the adversary's top echelons is certainly the correct direction, but it is not easy to implement nor does it guarantee full success. Improving one's own intelligence capabilities, especially in visual intelligence (VISINT), is essential but also provides only a partial solution. When all is said and done, the US certainly did not lack any VISINT, but it still made a grievous error of judgement, because these techniques are not capable of reading intentions in a direct way. VISINT is capable of reading intentions by analogy or indirectly.

Given the regrettable reality of strategic surprise and the concomitant initial military success achieved by the adversary in such a surprise, the way small states such as Israel can cope with such fateful and almost inevitable threats is by constantly maintaining as many military assets of permanent value, and above all, the crucially important element of strategic depth. (This is discussed further in Chapter 7.)

Other strategic intelligence blunders in the Second Gulf War involved overestimating Iraq's military might on the one hand and underestimating its nuclear programme on the other. It is no secret that, during the Kuwait crisis, the US wrongly assessed Iraq's army as the fourth largest and strongest in the world. This assessment stemmed from the numerical size of the Iraqi army and from the amount of military equipment and materiel at its disposal, as well as from Iraq having the upper hand over Iran in the First Gulf War.[8]

This assessment was mistaken. Numbers alone are not a true indication of actual military prowess. Combat performance is no less crucial a factor. Generally, a country's air force provides the best indication of the qualitative dimension of its military might yet, as we have already mentioned and as the US itself was aware, the Iraqi air force had not been overly successful in its combat operations in the First Gulf War. Likewise, in its offensive in the initial stage of the First Gulf War (1980–82), Iraqi ground forces did not succeed in capturing more than a small fraction of Khuzistan (essentially the objective of that war) and, finding itself unable to advance, eventually had to retreat back to Iraq's territory. It is true that in subsequent years (1982–88) the Iraqi army proved to have a rather good defensive capability; but this was demonstrated against a militarily non-professional, and insufficiently armed and equipped, adversary – Iran after the Khomeini revolution. Iraq also used exceptional and illegal weapons, such as chemical agents in its military operations – specifically, in its counter-attacks. Iraq did not really win the First Gulf War; it was more a case of Iran losing it.

There was also no sound reason for estimating that the Iraqis would be a serious match for the Coalition forces. The mistake in intelligence here could have been very costly; indeed, it came uncomfortably close to preventing the US from going to war against Iraq. If Iraq had indicated the slightest readiness to be more moderate, it is more than doubtful that the US would have resorted to war. Although some analysts might maintain that it is always preferable to exaggerate the enemy's strength, this approach has obvious shortcomings.

Underestimating Iraq's vast nuclear programme could also have had dire consequences. Hard-pressed to justify the possibility of going to war, the Administration underscored its assessment, in November 1990, that Iraq could attain operational nuclear capability in a relatively short time (some six months). This assessment, however, was more of an argument for domestic consumption – to be used against political adversaries who opposed going to war – than sound information. At the time, American intelligence knew almost nothing of the true dimensions of the Iraqi nuclear programme. These were only discovered after the war, as a result of one (or more) Iraqi nuclear scientist defecting to the West, and the subsequent UN inspection teams' revelations. This information led to the seizure of many enlightening documents on the programme in Baghdad after the war.[9] Most Iraqi non-conventional secrets were finally exposed when Saddam's minister in charge of all military industries defected to Jordan in August 1995. Saddam Hussein, fearing that his lies and non-compliance with UN demands would surface, hastened to come forward with many more confessions and documents about his non-conventional programmes.

The failure to correctly assess Iraq's nuclear programme meant, among other things, that if for some reason the US had refrained from going to war against Saddam in early 1991 – and this had almost been the case, due to the great misgivings of the Administration and other circles in the US about the war and the possibility that it might lead to a high casualty toll – it would have had to do so later, but under far worse conditions, against an Iraq with a nuclear capability.

From the standpoint of intelligence, it is important to stress the scope and dimension of Iraq's ambitious nuclear programme, and especially the extent to which the West was oblivious of it. Before the war the US had indeed noted that Iraq was likely to acquire nuclear weapons within a period of time ranging from six months to ten years. The former assessment was based on the assumption that Iraq would launch a crash programme and make illegal use of some 25 kg of safeguarded highly enriched uranium acquired with the reactors that it had purchased from France and the former Soviet Union, which were under (loose) supervision of the International Atomic Energy Agency (IAEA). The latter assessment was based on Iraq succeeding in producing her own enriched uranium and building atomic bombs in a systematic manner. Yet even after the war, there are still at least two different assessments: (a) that Iraq could have attained a nuclear capability in one-and-a-half to two years; and (b) that she could have attained it in not less than three to five years.[10]

The scope and size of Iraq's nuclear programme was a tremendous surprise to the international community. The country had a programme, previously altogether unknown and undetected, for enriching uranium by means of calutrons – in other words, by electromagnetic isotope separation (EMIS). This method of enriching uranium had been used by the US in the Manhattan Project in the Second World War, but was subsequently largely abandoned as obsolete. Not only did the West know nothing of this avenue in the Iraqi nuclear programme, but Iraq had made the most of its nuclear progress in this area.

Even though Iraqi plans and activities to enrich uranium by centrifuges were basically known, Western information on the centrifuge project turned out to be rather meagre.[11] Other significant and previously altogether unknown details about the Iraqi nuclear programme were discovered and to this day remain rather enigmatic. Iraq, for example, managed to produce a small amount (several grams) of plutonium, apparently from the Soviet reactor (IRT-5000) which it acquired in the 1970s. Documents also reveal that Iraq even planned to produce large quantities of lithium-6, used for manufacturing hydrogen bombs or for increasing the explosive force of regular atomic bombs. A small quantity of enriched uranium was discovered in the nuclear centre at Tuwaitha (the site of the Osirak reactor destroyed by the Israel Air Force in June 1981), perhaps indicating the existence of additional stockpiles that had been removed from that site.

If these disclosures have substance, one may wonder whether the Iraqis had already succeeded in producing highly enriched uranium, or whether they had received it from some other country.

The Iraqis, it appeared, had also made considerable progress in their weaponisation programme – in designing a nuclear bomb, based on an implosion-type device with a uranium core and an intended yield of about 20 kilotons. They were also working hard on the triggering system, essential for uniformly successful detonation of a nuclear bomb. Moreover, Iraq had already run some 20 tests of nuclear-related ultra-high explosives, of which virtually nothing was known.

It also turned out that Iraq had more sites related to her nuclear programme than were previously known too (at least 25). Even though many of these suspected sites were bombed in the war (although with only partial success), very little was known of what had actually been happening at these locations, especially at the important sites of Al-Atheer, Tarmiya, Al-Furat, Ash-sharqat, Al-Qaqa, Za'afraniya, and others (aside from the central nuclear site at Tuwaitha). The large number of sites points to an extensive, grandiose nuclear programme in line with Saddam's aspiration for rapid progress along a broad front, giving his nuclear plans greater flexibility and survivability. Ominously, most of it escaped the eyes of Western intelligence or was not understood for what it truly was.

The absence of such critical information raises at least two important issues concerning efforts at intelligence gathering. First, it makes one wonder about the value of supervision by the International Atomic Energy Agency (IAEA) in Vienna. Agency inspectors visited the French and Soviet Iraqi reactors twice a year, and were actually authorised to visit any other site of nuclear activity, yet their inspections were confined to these two legal reactors and even these did not reveal any illicit activity. It is interesting how they could have failed to observe that bomb-quality plutonium was being produced (albeit in very small quantities) at the Soviet reactor, as was revealed after the war. Second, one wonders how such important information regarding the Iraqi nuclear programme could have remained concealed from Western intelligence agencies when dozens of companies and hundreds of experts from Western Europe and elsewhere were involved in assisting Iraq in this programme. It is worrying that these companies, which assisted and traded with Iraq before the war, had probably not co-operated with the intelligence agencies after the war, and are most likely not co-operating even today. It is highly doubtful that they helped the Coalition's intelligence during the Kuwait crisis and the war, when any scrap of information on weapons of mass destruction was desperately sought in order to save the lives of their compatriots. Perhaps economic and political sensitivities led the governments of Western Europe to engage in a cover-up for this intelligence blunder. The continued difficulty with UN inspections in Iraq also stems primarily from lack of information.[12]

FAILINGS OF INTELLIGENCE DURING THE WAR

Even though a 42-day air battle and a sweeping 100-hour ground attack could not possibly have taken place without the necessary intelligence data, certain significant intelligence blunders were nevertheless evident at the operational level.[13] Intelligence in the Second Gulf War was mostly target intelligence and was largely based on information obtained from aerial photography, reconnaissance and battle damage assessment (BDA). Tactical combat intelligence also played an important role in the war, but there is a lack of appropriate information in this regard.

At least two major failures stand out with respect to tactical field intelligence. The first failure concerned the Iraqi attack on Khafji[14] that was not even detected until Iraqi units had already taken control of the town. A similar intelligence failure occurred when some 150 Iraqi aircraft, including 33 transport and other large planes (for intelligence and surveillance), began defecting to Iran (probably in broad daylight) with little, if any, air intervention by Coalition aircraft. Be that as it may, the focus here is on target intelligence and battle damage assessment, since this war can primarily be characterised as a massive air campaign.

Disclosures from Iraq after the war indicate considerable failings in target intelligence. These shortcomings were especially evident in two contexts which we have already discussed – fighting the mobile SSM launchers in western Iraq[15] and the air onslaught on sites for development and production of non-conventional weapons. It appears, however, that there were also quite a few other intelligence failings. The fact that a huge military object such as the super-gun at Jebel Hamriyan, in northern Iraq, with its 52-metre-long tube (and other large components) was not discovered by VISINT raises several questions regarding the expertise of American combat intelligence. It also appears that this intelligence was not sufficiently aware of the fact that the fixed-site missile launchers in western Iraq (some 28–30 of them) might be dummy launchers,[16] or that they might be less relevant to the missile launchings and operation. The great effort expended bombing them appears to have been pointless. It also appears that intelligence was not sufficiently alert to the movements of the mobile missile launchers from their original locations in the H-2 area (in western Iraq) to adjacent areas (such as Al-Kayim). In another regard, the scope and pace of the air offensive seemed to diminish during the last week or two of the war due to a shortage of strategic targets to be attacked. Yet two years later, ironically, the Americans had to launch another attack, involving dozens of cruise missiles, on the Iraqi nuclear facility at Za'afraniya.

The same criticism applies to battle damage assessment, as official American sources themselves admit.[17] This is especially unfortunate for, even though many targets were attacked and the Coalition air force had all the time and visual means needed to find out what damage had been incurred on the targets attacked, to learn which missions failed, and to correct the situation, this was not done – or at least was not done properly. One of the more obvious methods of obtaining accurate and effective BDA is to study in depth aerial photographs taken after an attack on the target and to decipher these photographs correctly, and not to rely solely on visual information obtained from sometimes rather off-hand, verbal debriefings of the pilots (according to which attacks on the target were almost always 'successful').

How could these blunders have occurred when the Coalition had such a clear advantage in technology and materiel, as well as good intelligence access to Iraq? The US deployed a wide variety of sophisticated intelligence means around the battle theatre. These included means deployed with the Central Command (CENTCOM) in charge of the battle arena: E-8J-STARS aircraft[18] with advanced radar systems capable of detecting troop and weapons movements on the ground; TR-1A planes, tactical reconnaissance aircraft; F-14-TARPS and RF-4C reconnaissance aircraft, primarily for aerial photography; Pioneer Remote Piloted Vehicles (RPVs, purchased from Israel), and of course also AWACS. Apart from these tools for gathering theatre intelligence, the CIA's and DIA's strategic intelligence tools, notably some ten satellites (KH-11s and others), provided communications and electronic data as well as aerial photographs. In short the Coalition had a wealth of VISINT and SIGINT[19] tools at its disposal.

The intelligence shortcomings during the war can be attributed to two main causes. First, it is clear almost beyond doubt that human intelligence (HUMINT) resources – human sources such as spies and secret agents – were deplorably lacking.[20] When all is said and done, even the most advanced visual equipment, including satellites, cannot provide a clear and unequivocal answer to intelligence dilemmas; moreover, they have certain inherent shortcomings, such as locating mobile objects or detecting objects screened from sight and from aerial photography. As we have mentioned, intentions and decisions cannot be discovered by aerial means, except indirectly (in which case one might also arrive at erroneous and far-fetched assessments), and partially by means of communications intelligence. The importance of human intelligence was clearly brought home for the first time when an Iraqi nuclear scientist defected and disclosed a wealth of information about Iraq's nuclear programme to American intelligence. Similarly, the August 1995 defection of Karmel Hussain (Saddam's son-in-law) provided a wealth of information on the Iraqi weapons programme.

The lack of intelligence, especially HUMINT, was no less striking in the fact that no Western intelligence body knew for sure of the existence of 30 chemical warheads for the al-Hussein missiles until Iraq herself admitted this. How Western intelligence agencies could have failed to extract this information from the hundreds of Western experts and technicians assisting Iraq in her non-conventional projects is perplexing. These foreign hostages could easily have been approached for questioning when they were released in

December 1990 (very close to the outbreak of the war). Their pieces of first-hand information could have been crucial to the war effort and particularly to the intelligence databank. Moreover, even if, for mistaken political reasons, American intelligence had not been interested in information about Iraq before the Kuwait crisis, this was no longer the case after early August 1990.[21]

A second reason for the failings of American (and Western) intelligence in the war was most likely failings or limited expertise in intelligence gathering and processing, including failures in the interpretation of aerial photographs and communications signals. An interesting example of an error in the interpretation of an aerial photograph occurred on 28 October 1992, when General Schwarzkopf showed a press conference a video that had been photographed by an F-15 and which ostensibly showed seven mobile Scud (al-Hussein) missile launchers being destroyed but in actual fact pictured fuel trucks moving from Jordan to Iraq, and definitely not missile launchers.[22] This, and similar errors, stemmed from lack of combat experience due largely to the US behaving and functioning as a superpower even in a non-superpower conflict. As a superpower, the US had put great emphasis on the doctrine of global war, and had prepared itself decades in advance for such an eventuality. Even when the US took six months to prepare for war against a Third World adversary (Iraq), its point of departure was still that of a superpower. This meant relying first and foremost on massive fire power and less on the finer tactical details of battle conduct and management. In other words, as a superpower, the US was not sufficiently doctrinally prepared for this sort of war and also lacked the necessary tactical sophistication.[23]

Yet, in contrast to previous wars, the US army did show greater sophistication and laudable professionalism in the operational-tactical sphere but this was only a relative change for the better. When it came to combat engagement, the same inherent problems surfaced, notably a lack of operational-tactical expertise in wars involving Third World opponents. This will have to change and improve if the US wishes to obtain better results in the future. Real-time intelligence and intelligence capability gathering, processing, and disseminating information are key factors for success in war, even for a super-power.[24]

The above discussion does not necessarily have direct or specific implications for Israel since the IDF is better skilled in intelligence, if only due to its extensive combat experience, culled over many years in wars and confrontations of a type foreign to a superpower such as the US. Nevertheless, it is important that Israel learn from every wartime experience, even if it is marked by shortcomings. It is equally important for Israel to be aware of the intelligence capabilities and limitations of her superpower ally, especially when that ally goes to war against one of its enemies since reducing the power of this enemy is closely related to the scope of the ally's information about the former's arsenals and potential as well as the latter's ability to exploit this information successfully on the battle-field.

ISRAELI INTELLIGENCE

Israeli intelligence was also somewhat taken by surprise by the outbreak of the crisis and Iraq's invasion of Kuwait, although less so than Western intelligence organisations.[25] Israeli intelligence also suffered from a lack of information, although under the circumstances it was reasonably well informed about Iraq and her military strength. It made some unfortunate errors in assessing Saddam's threats against Israel and in its information on vital details, such as the specific location of Iraq's mobile missile launchers, whether the missiles were equipped with chemical warheads, and even more significant, the effect that the missiles would have on Israel. Similarly, it was conjectured that Iraqi aircraft might dare to launch direct attacks on objectives in Israel, or that Iraq might dispatch a ground and air expeditionary force to Jordan and attack Israel from there. The assessment that Saddam Hussein would not be deterred from using chemical warfare against Israel also proved incorrect.

It should have been obvious from the outset, and not only with hindsight, that these assessments were highly exaggerated. Iraq, after all, found herself threatened on all sides:[26] from the south and the north (Saudi Arabia and Turkey) by the Coalition; from the East by Iran, which Iraq could not trust to refrain from taking advantage of the situation; and from the west by Syria, led by Saddam's sworn opponent, Assad. Given such a situation, it was unrealistic to believe that Iraq would have the power to engage in a real confrontation against the distant state of Israel too. It is, however, normal for intelligence to present all possible threats so that, among other things, it is not accused after the fact of having failed to warn of a particular danger. This is especially true when, from the outset, information on the enemy is narrowly based and rather scarce and is periodically coupled with very serious threats voiced by that foe.

Although Israeli intelligence was not free from errors and shortcomings in the Second Gulf War, it was still better than other intelligence services in its provision of information and assessments.[27] This was so because, from the outset, Israel was more sensitive to the threats emanating from Iraq in general and against itself in particular. This sensitivity was only heightened by Saddam's threat in early April 1990, 'to incinerate half of Israel with binary chemical weapons'. By that time Israel was aware of the SSM array being built in western Iraq and of the growing military and intelligence co-operation between Iraq and Jordan. These and other worries prompted the visit of former Defence Minister Moshe Arens to the US in July 1990 (about a month before Iraq invaded Kuwait) accompanied by the heads of Israeli intelligence. The Minister of Defence and the Israeli intelligence organisations were ill at ease about Iraq's extensive nuclear endeavour and its aggressive intentions.

It is understandable that Israeli intelligence may have suffered from insufficient information, especially visual information, about Iraq. After all, it did not have the wealth of means for intelligence gathering or the relatively easy access to Arab states and their populations that Western intelligence agencies enjoyed. Moreover, the geographical distance between Israel and the heart of Iraq (about 1,000 km) was a particularly significant factor impeding steadily flowing collection of visual and communications intelligence. Recruiting and employing human sources in Iraq was far from easy for Israeli intelligence organisations due to the absence of a common border. A small state such as Israel faces fundamental problems in the field of intelligence, in determining collection priorities for its limited resources. It is logical for these resources to be applied in the first instance to bordering confrontational states. Moreover, even if one wishes to alter priorities, changes cannot be made instantly – and certainly not when they involve recruiting and managing human resources. (Incidentally, the same holds for larger and richer states than Israel.)

One of the basic ways of improving Israeli intelligence, especially with respect to a country such as Iraq and distant and dangerous countries such as Iran and Libya, is to acquire satellite capabilities and perhaps also use long-range RPVs. Israel actually began a satellite programme long before the outbreak of the Second Gulf War. The war only lent renewed and poignant expression to the need for the programme and probably accelerated its progress.[28] When this and other programmes are complete, they will primarily facilitate the gathering of visual intelligence, but they will not be able to provide advance warning of missile launchings since, to do so, a country needs geosynchronous satellites, something only available to superpowers. When these and similar facilities are put into operation they will vastly enhance Israel's visual intelligence capability in terms of collection from distant countries which today pose a more direct and greater threat to Israel than in the past, especially by means of missiles and long-range fire power. Nevertheless, even these visual means of gathering intelligence, and other similar ones, will not be able to overcome their inherent limitations and do away with the need for human intelligence, or take the place of correct assessments. Paradoxically, additional raw information increases background noise, making it harder to filter in order to obtain accurate intelligence assessments; still, additional raw information remains absolutely essential.

Another issue that surfaced for the first time in the Second Gulf War was the extent to which Israeli intelligence depended on outside sources. This was most pronounced in its dependence on US early warnings of SSM launchings. It is nothing new for friendly intelligence organisations to exchange items of information or assessments, either on an *ad hoc* or a regular basis. This is generally done out of sober considerations of expediency, on a give-and-take basis. Indeed, no intelligence organisation can be altogether self-sufficient in its collection efforts or its supply of information; it is only natural that gaps be filled in and missing pieces of information be supplied by means of free trade in intelligence exchange. The situation in the Second Gulf War, however, was quite different: Israeli intelligence was heavily dependent on the US in a specific realm. For Israeli intelligence to be completely in the dark and totally dependent with respect to a specific and crucial area of information was a new and unsound situation which Israeli decision makers must take care to remedy.

Although Israel will always have gaps in its intelligence information, because financial resources and other capabilities are limited, it must never find itself in a condition where it lacks essential information. Israel's efforts to develop an intelligence satellite and long-range RPVs and other means are crucial in remedying such a situation. The need for such research and development was clearly manifest after the war, but must be kept well in mind as the 'peace process' progresses, since the latter is likely to diminish Israel's willingness to mobilise her limited financial resources to support ambitious defence projects.

NOTES

1. Cf. *JDW*, 14 December 1991; *Ma'ariv Report*, pp. 25, 29. The 'Pentagon Report', ibid., also specifically admits a 'shortcoming in strategic intelligence'.
2. Cf. *Ma'ariv Report* (chapter on intelligence); Mubarak also repeated this in a

speech about a year after the war ('You deceived us all...'), cited in *Ma'ariv*, 4 March 1992.

3. Cf. the leak of Moshe Arens' remarks in the Knesset Committee on Foreign and Security Affairs that, 'Israeli intelligence must do some soul-searching'.
4. Cf. IAF Head of Intelligence Research Branch on the 'deeply ingrained concepts,' *Hamanit* (the Israel Intelligence Corps journal), April 1991.
5. Cf. E. Kam, 'Strategic Surprise and the Gulf War', in *Studies in Israel's Security Doctrine* (Ramat Gan: BESA Center for Strategic Studies, Bar-Ilan University, August 1991).
6. On this conversation and similar remarks by former Assistant Secretary of State John Kelley, cf. *Ma'ariv Report*, p. 17, and the testimony before the Senate given by Ms April Gillespie, then US Ambassador to Iraq (cited in *Davar*, 21 March 1991).
7. Cf. Senator J. Biden, 'Statement before the Senate Foreign Relations Committee', 23 October 1991. See also the 'Air Survey', ibid., which points to the absence of intelligence on Iraq before 2 August 1990.
8. The assessment of Iraq's army as the fourth largest in the world also appears in the 'Pentagon Report,' ibid., even one year after the war.
9. Cf. several articles on the subject, providing a wealth of information: D. Albright and M. Hibbs, 'Iraq's Bomb: Blueprints and Artifacts', *Bulletin of Atomic Scientists*, January–February 1992; Gary Milhollin, 'Building Saddam', *The New York Times Magazine*, 8 March 1992; L. Spector, 'Nuclear Proliferation in the Middle East', *Orbis*, Spring 1992; and D. Albright and H. Hibbs, 'Iraq's Quest for the Nuclear Grail: What Can We Learn', *Arms Control Today*, July–August 1992; Maurizio Zifferero, 'The IAEA: Neutralizing Iraq's Nuclear Weapons Potential', *Arms Control Today*, April 1993; Tim Trevan, 'UNSCOM Faces Entirely New Verification Challenges in Iraq', *Arms Control Today*, April 1993; D. Albright, 'A Proliferation Primer', *Bulletin of Atomic Scientists*, June 1993. More updated information is in two important articles: D. Albright and R. Kelley, 'Has Iraq Come Clean At Last?' *The Bulletin of the Atomic Scientists*, November/December 1995; D. Albright and R. Kelley, 'Massive Programs, Meager Results', ibid.
10. Cf. the articles cited above, as well as *Davar*, 21 May 1992, citing the *New York Times* statement that experts concluded that Iraq needed at least three more years to obtain the bomb.
11. On the eve of the war, Iraq had between eight and 30 calutrons. (At least 80 are needed to produce enough fissionable material for a bomb.) On the other hand, defects were found in the method of uranium enrichment using centrifuges. Cf. *JDW*, 25 January 1992, and the articles cited above.
12. Rolf Ekeus, head of the UN Special Commission for detecting and eliminating non-conventional weapons and ballistic missiles, was instructive in his remarks on the mystery of Iraqi uranium enrichment by means of centrifuges and the lack of intelligence in this regard (*Ma'ariv*, 28 May 1992). Also cf. the article by the head of the International Atomic Energy Agency, Hans Blix, 'Verification of Nuclear Proliferation: The Lessons of Iraq', *Washington Quarterly*, Autumn 1992.
13. Cf. E. Ben-Nun in *Ma'ariv*, 19 June 1992; and the 'Pentagon Report'.
14. On the Khafji incident (lack of information, poor co-ordination and units

of the Marines being bombed by American aircraft, etc.) cf. *Ha'aretz*, 23 February 1991.

15. General Schwarzkopf: 'We went into this business [eliminating the SSMs – A. L.] with grossly mistaken intelligence estimates. Another possibility is that the pilots lied, but I tend to believe the former possibility.' Cited in *Ma'ariv*, 28 February 1991.
16. On this and on Iraqi dummies in general, cf. *Bamahane*, 19 September 1991.
17. The 'Pentagon Report', which is the official report on the war, explicitly admits this. It is also admitted in the 'Air Survey'.
18. J-STARS is the Joint Services Tactical Acquisition and Reconnaissance System.
19. Signal Intelligence (SIGINT) consisted of Communication Intelligence (COMINT) and Electronic Intelligence (ELINT).
20. Cf. the remarks by the then CIA Director, Robert M. Gates, cited in *Yediot Aharonot*, 23 January 1992; and *Newsweek*, 20 January 1992. The 'Pentagon Report' also mentions a lack of Arabic speakers, etc.
21. The 'Air Survey', ibid., admits that US knowledge of targets within Iraq was 'sketchy' and that the amount of 'valid targets grew by nearly 50 per cent between 2 August, 1990 and 16 January, 1991'.
22. Experts realised later that they were actually fuel trucks. See also General Schwarzkopf's remarks to the *New York Times*, cited in *Ha'aretz*, 6 February 1991.
23. This observation is also mentioned in the 'Air Survey'.
24. Cf. the reference to this by Brigadier General E. Eilam, head of the Research and Development Authority, Israeli Ministry of Defence (*Ma'ariv*, 12 May 1991).
25. Cf. *Ma'ariv Report* (chapter on intelligence).
26. A. Levran, 'The Threat of Missiles and Chemical Weapons', *Ma'ariv*, 14 August 1990; A. Levran, 'The Experts are Drowning in Figures', *Hadashot*, 13 September 1990; A. Levran, 'Masks May Give Saddam Dangerous Ideas', *Jerusalem Post*, 12 October 1990.
27. Cf. *Ma'ariv Report* (chapter on intelligence), p. 13; also cf. E. Kam, *Studies in Israel's Security Doctrine*, ibid.
28. Former Minister of Defence Arens to *Ma'ariv*, 16 August 1991; also *Ma'ariv Report* (chapter on intelligence). On long-range RPVs, cf. Arens in an interview to the *AFJI*, cited in *Ma'ariv*, 6 August 1991.

4

Iraq Refraining from Chemical Warfare: Reasons and Implications

Iraq had used chemical weapons in the First Gulf War. Saddam Hussein had uttered explicit threats, on 2 April 1990, 'to incinerate half of Israel with binary chemical weapons,'[1] and, in December 1990, to respond to an American attack by using a secret weapon – specifically a chemical weapon.[2] These facts heightened the apprehension that the Second Gulf War, more than any previous regional war, might become a non-conventional confrontation. Since this did not occur, one must ask why Saddam did not use non-conventional weapons against Israel and the Coalition forces in this conflict. It must be said, however, that addressing the hypothetical question of why a certain development did not take place isn't a simple matter.

REASONS FOR IRAQ NOT USING CHEMICAL WEAPONS

It is somewhat easier to understand why biological and nuclear weapons (as opposed to chemical weapons) were not used in this war. Iraq did not yet possess these types of weapons – at least not on an operational level. Indeed, Iraq repeatedly reported to the UN that she did not possess any of these types of weapons at all. Even if Iraq's report was false with regard to biological weapons (for it appears it had 'something' at least in this field, particularly anthrax), this does not mean that it possessed fully operational biological agents. Iraq certainly did not have operational nuclear weapons at its disposal, although, as we have learned, it had taken the first steps towards their development.

Iraq not only possessed an arsenal of chemical agents, but had even used them extensively against Iran and the Kurds in the First Gulf War. Furthermore, after the Second Gulf War, Iraq admitted to having 30 al-Hussein surface-to-surface missiles equipped with chemical warheads, in addition to a rather huge chemical stockpile of thousands of artillery shells and aerial bombs filled with mustard and nerve gas (sarin and taboon) and with a binary mode of operation (in other words they consisted of a mixture of two types of gas to increase their impact, or were built separately from the main warhead to enhance safety). It turned out later that Iraq's stockpiles of these weapons were more than four times greater than initially reported.[3] Thus there is ample reason to ask why Saddam Hussein did not resort to chemical weapons in the Second Gulf War.

Israeli concern, of course, focuses more on the existence of al-Hussein missiles equipped with chemical warheads than on Iraq's general stockpile of artillery shells or aerial bombs. This is because of their innovative nature (they did not yet exist in the First Gulf War), and because these missiles, more than fighter planes, could enable Iraq to strike at Israel if it so desired, and to do so with relative ease. Of course the Coalition forces were also highly concerned about Iraq's chemical artillery shells; yet it is important to note here that no proof of any intention or actual preparations to use such shells against the Coalition forces was found in the field after Kuwait's liberation. Thus, beyond the question of why Saddam Hussein did not use chemical weapons against the Coalition, a more specific and crucial question remains: why did he not use chemical al-Hussein missiles against Israel in the Second Gulf War? A preliminary response to this question could have been that it did not have such weapons in her possession; however, according to Iraq's own reports, this assessment turns out to have been unfounded. Since Iraq has proven to be unreliable in general, and specifically in its reports to the UN concerning its non-conventional arsenal, it may well be that it possessed even more chemical missile warheads than stated. Incidentally, the Iraqi government reported that its own personnel had themselves destroyed some 40 chemical missiles (the exact types of missiles are unknown). Even if Iraq had at its disposal over 30 (or even 70) chemical missiles, this still does not say much about whether they were operationally fit or efficacious.[4]

Even if some of the chemical missile warheads were binary this still does not mean that they had optimal detonation mechanisms, or anything other than impact fuses. With impact fuses, the gas disperses when the missile's warhead hits the ground, but its dispersion is about as half as effective as with proximity fuses, which explode the warheads at a suitable, specifically planned altitude above the target area and greatly enhance the efficiency of gas dispersion over the target.[5] Similarly, there is no certain indication that the Iraqis tested al-Hussein missiles equipped with chemical warheads nor, more importantly, that they had found an adequate solution to the problem of an operational warhead fuse for efficiently dispersing chemical agents.

With all these technical and operational difficulties, it is still hard to say whether Saddam Hussein refrained from launching chemical SSMs at Israel because of these practical obstacles alone. To answer our question, therefore, we must seek other explanations.

One possibility is that, even though Israel did not deter Saddam Hussein from attacking it with missiles equipped with conventional warheads, it still managed to deter him from using chemical weapons. Indeed, the argument that Saddam was deterred by Israel's potential nuclear superiority[6] is logically valid, even if it is impossible to prove. It should be noted that when Saddam threatened Israel on 2 April 1990, stating that he would 'incinerate half of Israel' he qualified his threat with the stipulation that this would occur should Iraq first be attacked by nuclear weapons.

During the Second Gulf War there were at least two opportunities to remind Saddam Hussein of Israel's nuclear potential. On 2 February 1991, Secretary of Defense Richard Cheney was asked by a CNN interviewer why Saddam Hussein had thus far refrained from using chemical warfare against Israel. He responded that the reason might have to do with the fear of Israeli retaliation using non-conventional weapons. When Israeli Minister of Defence Moshe Arens was asked in an NBC interview the following day to comment on Cheney's response, he said that 'the Secretary did not explicitly mention a nuclear response, but if the implication is that Saddam has reason to be concerned, he had better be concerned'.[7] Thus, it might have been clear to Saddam Hussein that, as far as Israel was concerned, chemical warfare would entail different rules of the game.

Indeed, sharp retorts had been voiced in Israel to Saddam's threat to incinerate half the country and these had surely come to Saddam's attention. Yitzhak Rabin, then Minister of Defence, said at the time that, 'It is within our power to respond with a blow many times more crushing.'[8] Professor Yuval Ne'eman, then Minister of Science and Energy, responded in December 1990: 'We have an excellent response; and that is to threaten Saddam with the same merchandise.' If this did not suffice, then the comment made on the eve of the war by Lieutenant General Dan Shomron, then Chief of the IDF General Staff, that 'we will not be the first to use nuclear weapons,'[9] conveyed a weighty message (although this was probably a slip of the tongue).

Although fear of non-conventional Israeli retaliation might have deterred Saddam Hussein from using chemical SSMs to a certain degree, in our opinion, a more comprehensive answer to the question of why he failed to use them must be sought in the broader spectrum of deterrence, on the one hand, and in Iraqi patterns of chemical warfare in the First Gulf War (against Iran) on the other.

When we analyse Iraqi patterns of employing chemical weapons in the First Gulf War (in which, as we have mentioned, chemical agents were used only in aerial bombs and artillery shells), we see that although Saddam Hussein brazenly defied international prohibitions and ignored his own commitments, such as the Geneva Protocol of 1925, to which Iraq is a signatory, he still did so with a measure of self-restraint, imposing substantial restrictions on himself.[10] In the war against Iran, as a general rule, Iraq used chemical agents only for defensive purposes, in order to repulse Iranian forces that had invaded its territory and that were threatening to shatter critical defensive lines. This had been the Iraqi's mode of operation since 1983, when they began using chemical warfare against the Iranians, and it continued to be the general pattern for a considerable length of time (throughout five years of war).

The same rule was also applied when Iraq began using chemical warfare against its own Kurdish citizens in April 1987. The motive behind this action was that, for years, most of the Iraqi Kurds had been collaborating closely with Iraq's bitter foe, Iran, and were actually disrupting Iraqi troop movements and war operations in the northern regions of the country. Thus, from Baghdad's point of view, these Kurds could be considered enemies, perhaps even as Iranian soldiers on Iraqi soil. However, both in its actions against the Iranians and against the Kurds, Iraq restricted its use of chemical weapons solely to within its own territory and borders.

Occasionally chemical munition slipped out near, or across, the border and front line, but Iraq never employed chemical weapons against military or civilian targets deep within Iranian territory proper. Since the world in general, and especially the US, did not initiate any harsh sanctions against Iraq for using this proscribed weaponry (at most, it occasionally deplored Iraq's chemical warfare), Iraq became increasingly audacious regarding the circumstances and methods in which it used it. Nevertheless, until the end of that war in the summer of 1988, Iraq did not dare exceed the restrictive parameters of using chemical warfare solely for defensive purposes and only within its own territory. This is instructive because Iraq could have justified escalating its use of chemical weapons against Iran, since the latter was considered a fanatical, pariah state by most countries of the world. More importantly, Iraq could have had the audacity to use chemical weapons repeatedly and even escalate its chemical warfare since, practically until the end of the war, Iran did not possess any significant non-conventional weapons to deter Iraq or with which to respond in kind.

We observe, therefore, that Iraq's self-restraint in using chemical agents did not stem from the kindness of Saddam's heart, nor from his adversary's deterrent (which was virtually non-existent), but rather from the fact that, from the outset, crossing the critical threshold of using non-conventional weapons is neither simple nor is it to be taken lightly; the use of non-conventional weapons must be tailored to very specific circumstances.

On this basis one could say that if Saddam Hussein saw fit to impose limitations on himself in the use of chemical weapons in such mitigating circumstances as pertained in the First Gulf War, he would surely refrain from using these weapons in far graver circumstances. Indeed, in the Second Gulf War these mitigating circumstances did not pertain as far as Iraq was concerned. In this war Saddam confronted adversaries that he knew to be equipped with even more lethal weapons that could deliver him a double dose of his own medicine. But, above all else, in the Second Gulf War (in contrast to the First Gulf War) Saddam Hussein probably realised that by using chemical weapons he would be writing a death warrant for himself and his régime. Hence, the common pre-war assumption that Saddam would use chemical weapons against Israel simply because he had already made intensive use of such weapons once before, in the First Gulf War, proved unfounded.[11]

Using non-conventional weapons, including chemical weapons, is no trifling matter; it involves crossing a critical threshold and is based upon serious deliberations. This is certainly true when speaking of 'rules of the game' between adversaries with a powerful and similar military potential. Therefore, the assessment by US Vice-President Dan Quayle that, 'since Iraq has already used chemical warfare once, we believe that she may do so in this war, as well', or of the French Chief of General Staff and sources in the British General Staff that 'the ground battle will be conducted in a chemical environment', certainly proved unfounded.[12]

As a general rule, a nation will reserve non-conventional weapons for the most dire and exceptional circumstances, for what we may call an 'extreme distress scenario', where it is on the verge of military defeat and national collapse. One cannot simply accept the general assumption that, since a certain adversary has already used chemical warfare in the past, he will do so again in another war; rather, each case must be closely scrutinised according to the specific circumstances, bearing in mind that use of non-conventional weapons is not the rule. When we analyse the handful of instances in which chemical weapons were employed since the First World War, we observe, interestingly, that they were always used between adversaries who were markedly unequal in their military potential or their international status. This was the case in the two prominent examples in the Middle East: Egypt's use of chemical weapons against rebel tribes in Yemen in the mid-1960s, and Iraq's use against Iran in 1983–88 (and against its own Kurds in 1987–88). This was also the case in other parts of the world where chemical warfare was reputedly used: by Soviet forces against the Mujahedin rebels in the war in Afghanistan, by the Cubans against the UNITA rebels in Angola, and in Libya's war against Chad. In all these cases chemical weapons were used against second rate adversaries that had almost no international status and certainly had no chemical (or similar) weapons with which they could respond or deter their attackers. When chemical warfare was employed in relatively backwoods regions, international censure and sanctions could be easily avoided.

Several Arab countries turned to the development and production of chemical weapons in the first place as a means of counterbalancing Israel's nuclear potential. The Arabs may have reduced their helplessness against Israel in the non-conventional arms sphere by adding chemical weapons to their arsenal; but they must nevertheless surely be aware of the asymmetry which still persists in the destructive power and impact of these two different arsenals. Proof of this lies in the fact that there are also Arab states still striving to obtain nuclear weapons while at the same time calling for non-conventional disarmament of the Middle East – specifically for a Nuclear Weapon Free Zone. More significantly, even though Egypt and Syria had chemical weapons at their disposal in the 1967 and 1973 wars, in which they were defeated (the 1973 war ending with Israeli forces 100 km from Egypt's capital and 40 km from Syria's capital), they refrained from using these weapons against Israel or against Israeli armed forces advancing on their own territory.

Some analysts believe that certain Arab states may be tempted to use chemical weapons against Israel in order to cause it heavy casualties and assure themselves military gains (at least initially), especially if they assume that Israel will not dare retaliate with more potent weapons. This view, however, is somewhat simplistic. There is no guarantee to the Arabs that Israel will indeed refrain from escalating if attacked by such horrible weapons as chemical agents. An Israeli response 'in the same currency' might deter its opponents from resorting to chemical warfare. Furthermore, regional rulers must be well aware of the grave significance of using poison gas against Jews and Israelis after the Second World War and the Holocaust.

We may therefore presume that the regional states will be in no rush to use non-conventional weapons, including chemical warfare – as illustrated by the wars mentioned (1967, 1973, and 1991) – except under very dire circumstances and conditions of acute distress. In the Second Gulf War Saddam Hussein may indeed have been on the verge of such a situation when he suffered a severe military defeat and the humiliation of his forces being routed in Kuwait and crushed on the battlefield in southern Iraq; but Saddam was sufficiently wise to curb himself and pretend that his defeat was not so terrible. Above all, he knew that the survival of his régime and his own person had not yet been critically endangered, and that most of Iraq had not yet been devastated.

Thus, despite Saddam's repeated explicit threats to use chemical weapons against Israel and the Coalition, and despite his military defeat, these threats were not realised because the capital, Baghdad, most of the territory of Iraq, and the majority of his vitally important forces had survived the ordeal of the war and were under control. In other words, he and his country were not facing total collapse nor were they cornered in a situation of extreme distress. And so, Saddam Hussein did not let the chemical genie out of the bottle in the Second Gulf War. This behaviour on the part of Saddam could serve as a model for other regional leaders at war with Israel.

To complete this discussion, something must be said about the partial protective measures adopted by Israel and the Coalition forces and their influence on Iraq's decision not to use chemical weapons in the war. Operational research and simulation analysis show that the better protected the party attacked by chemical weapons, the smaller its losses.[13] Hence, given that Israel and the Coalition forces were protected by gas-mask kits and other measures, and that almost the only way of mounting a chemical attack on Israel was by chemical SSM warheads – and since Iraqi missiles were fired only at night, when Israel's population was indoors, protected in hermetically-sealed rooms – there was not much point in employing chemical weapons and thereby risking terrible retribution. Saddam Hussein might have taken this into consideration when he refrained from using chemical weapons against Israel.

It is, however, highly doubtful whether Israel's protective measures, and Saddam's own confinement to night-time attacks were the only factors convincing him to refrain from chemical warfare. He continued firing conventional SSMs at Israel many days after it must have been evident to him that Israel would not be dragged into war. The continued SSM fire appears to have been more an expression of deep hostility towards Israel and a desire to settle accounts with it, than the result of purely utilitarian considerations. Perhaps, by continuing to launch missiles at Israel, he believed that he would be able to make it reverse its posture of forbearance; yet he must surely have noted the declarations by the leaders of Egypt and Syria that if Israel should respond they would show understanding and not break up the Coalition.[14] Hence, the decision to continue firing at Israel could not have been purely utilitarian, but if it was a question of hostility, once Saddam realised that conventional SSMs were not causing Israel significant losses, and were not changing its strategic stance by drawing it into the war, then chemical warheads might actually have realised his strategic objectives.

When we examined Iraq's use of chemical weapons against Iranian forces, we observed that although Iran was better protected against chemical warfare from year to year, its losses nevertheless continued to rise.[15] However there is a significant difference between using chemical weapons against Iranian forces on the open battlefield and firing SSMs with chemical warheads at a relatively protected population in Israel. In our opinion, the major reason for Saddam Hussein failing to employ chemical weapons against Israel was that, in contrast to the First Gulf War, he never contemplated using them from the outset since he was aware that using non-conventional weapons in 'normal' conditions would entail different rules of the game. In addition, he was deterred by the might of his opponents.

ISRAEL'S MISTAKEN CHEMICAL PROTECTION POLICY

Another important question arises with respect to Iraqi restraint in the use of chemical weapons: did distributing gas masks and self-protection kits to Israel's population do more strategic harm than good? While distribution of protection kits indeed offered Israel's population a measure of protection given the conditions of the Second Gulf War, in our opinion it also caused harm. It implicitly legitimised the use of chemical weapons by Saddam Hussein and possibly also by other regional rulers in future wars against Israel. More significantly, it legitimised the use of such terrible weapons against Israel's civilian population and home front.[16] By distributing gas masks, Israel essentially signalled implicit acceptance of the possibility that chemical weapons might be used against its population, as if these were simply another type of conventional weapon or a logical development of regional warfare. If, from the beginning, Saddam had no intention of using chemical weapons against Israel for the various reasons discussed above, then distributing gas masks might have made him think that Israel was actually prepared to come to terms with chemical attacks on its population.

On the other hand, if Israel's inhabitants had not been provided with gas masks, then only its net deterrence posture would have come into play. More specifically, this would have conveyed a threefold, although clear, message: (a) that under no conditions would Israel be willing to come to terms with the use of non-conventional weapons; (b) that Israel certainly would not tolerate their being used against its sensitive population centres; and (c) that Israel would even be willing to take a great calculated risk in this regard.

Israel's political and military leaders, however, were unwilling to shoulder responsibility for Israeli inhabitants being hurt in chemical missile attacks (and we do not envy or disrespect these leaders for their difficult decision). This indicated an implicit acceptance of the possibility that there might be a dangerous change in the rules of the game in future wars with the Arab states. It is our suggestion that there is still scope for a major about-face in Israeli policy regarding chemical protection to a position that under no conditions would Israel be willing to agree to new rules of the game that include use of non-conventional weapons, especially against non-combatants, in future regional confrontations.

In summary, Saddam Hussein did not use chemical weapons in the Second Gulf War because he was deterred by his adversaries' superiority in non-conventional weapons, and because he probably never intended to use such weapons from the start. He was aware that different rules of the game pertain when the adversaries are equally matched, and he had already shown self-restraint in his use of chemical weapons in the First Gulf War. Hence, we may conclude that his non-use of chemical weapons in the Second Gulf War was neither accidental nor miraculous. This certainly bodes well for the future.

A related question concerns the validity of the strange but widespread fear that continues to plague many in Israel, even after the war, whenever political crises and tests of power erupt between Saddam Hussein and the UN, that Iraq might still attack Israel with chemical missiles. The main examples of such crises were in September 1991, when UN observers were detained for a while in a parking lot in Baghdad with documents they had seized about Iraq's nuclear programme; in August 1992, when the 'no fly zone', prohibiting Iraqi flights south of the 32nd parallel, was enforced; and in January 1993, when Iraq, taking advantage of President Bush reaching the end of his term of office, attempted to violate flight restrictions and other ceasefire limitations. If the lessons of the Second Gulf War are analysed correctly, however, it can be shown that such fears of Iraqi activity are basically unfounded.

One of the reasons for these apprehensions has to do with Saddam's image as an irrational ruler, as someone who will do whatever he pleases. For all his megalomania and provocative behaviour, however, Saddam Hussein is a rational ruler. The test of rationality among rulers and decision-makers involves several criteria: the extent to which their decisions take important facts into account, whether they perceive reality reasonably, whether they set reasonable objectives and employ logical methods to accomplish them, whether they consider cost-effectiveness, and the extent to which they alter policy and their behaviour in the event of an error or necessity. Saddam Hussein appears to stand the test in most of these regards.

Saddam Hussein proved his rationality on several occasions in decisions that were far from easy for him. First, he did not use chemical weapons in the Second Gulf War and did not even prepare to do so in Kuwait, notwithstanding his outspoken threats and ignominious defeat. Second, after the war Saddam realised that he had been vanquished and could not continue to confront the US and the UN militarily, hence his submissiveness to the UN decisions despite his own severe personal humiliation and the continued infringement of his country's sovereignty (the existence of a Kurdish enclave under UN supervision, flight prohibitions over northern and southern Iraq, repeated and intrusive inspections, harsh economic sanctions, destruction of his non-conventional arms and facilities, and so forth). Saddam's subterfuge of the UN should be viewed neither as irrational behaviour nor as a provocation, but rather as an attempt to rid himself of these embarrassing restrictions and as a result of his need to survive or at least retain his dignity before his own entourage and other influential domestic circles. We are by no means attempting to justify the behaviour of the Baghdad ruler (whose removal, incidentally, should have been one of the objectives during the war or thereafter), but rather to indicate that the motives for his policies and behaviour were not completely irrational.

Although Saddam is a harsh ruler, he is one whose actions are still rational. In the summer of 1982, when he concluded that his army's invasion of the Khuzistan region of Iran had failed, he did not hesitate to order a full retreat of his forces back to Iraqi territory. In the years that followed, almost until the end of the First Gulf War, he repeatedly appealed to Iran and the world to negotiate a ceasefire, because he realised that the war had become too costly to bear. During these years he also did all he could to ease the burden of the war on his country by renewing relations with his former adversaries, Egypt (despite the Camp David Accords) and the US. He even made a tactical change of tune regarding Israel and ceased to call for her annihilation in the traditional Ba'athist spirit (to the extent that some leading figures in Israel were ensnared and even sought to open channels to Iraq – to the resentment of the US administration).

Saddam Hussein undoubtedly made grave errors in implementing his policies. Miscalculations, however, are the lot of many rulers and are not an expression of dangerous irrationality. Saddam may have been far off the mark in his assessment of certain situations, as in his invasion of Iran in 1980, in his inflexibility regarding US warnings prior to and during the amassing of Coalition forces after his invasion of Kuwait, in his failure to correctly read the significance of the crumbling of the Soviet Union, and in his transferring some 150 planes to Iran (of all places) during the war. This does not, however, mean that he is incapable of halting or retreating when on the brink of overstepping the mark. Moreover, in all the examples cited, his considerations were not totally inconsequential nor was his reasoning unrealistic.

Another reason for the concern among Israelis about post-war chemical missile attacks is that Iraq was known to lie regarding its stockpiles of weapons of mass destruction and long-range SSMs. However, the fact that Iraq may well be concealing at least part of this war materiel does not necessarily mean it will make repeated or effective use of it in Baghdad's present condition. There are several good reasons for this. First, firing conventional SSMs, or particularly chemical ones, at Israel and Saudi Arabia (the Coalition's base) is not in Iraq's interest today. Quite the contrary – her interest is to cut down the dimensions of the lingering conflict and to reduce tensions with the UN and especially with the US. Furthermore, Iraqi SSM launchings can only induce the US to resort to military means again (primarily from the air) in order to complete the work that was left undone in the Second Gulf War, including renewed attacks on strategic objectives and government centres in Baghdad and its environs, and even on Saddam in person. Saddam is aware that, after the war, he is no match for the US and cannot afford to broaden his confrontation with it, even if the US Army has considerably reduced its ORBAT in the Persian Gulf.

Saddam Hussein has blatantly defied his adversaries on more than one occasion since the war; yet it is clear to him that if another confrontation were to flare up with them, he could not do much in terms of an actual response (as had been the case during the war itself). His outspoken words to the US and the UN win him points among his immediate circles in Iraq (and in the eyes of many other Arabs), where he is viewed as a fearless leader who dares to stand up to a superpower and defy a world organisation. Nor is such behaviour exceptional in Arab history and culture, where bravado is actually considered an asset.

Second, during the Second Gulf War Saddam had an important rational strategic objective in firing missiles at Israel, namely to break up the broad Coalition that was fighting him, and especially to put pressure on its Arab partners to withdraw. Such considerations are not relevant after the war because Syria and Egypt are not actively involved in the American struggle against Saddam and, in fact, are generally critical of US policy on Iraq. As for Saudi Arabia and Kuwait, they are still providing military bases for the US, and whether or not Saddam makes a military response involving SSMs against Israel is clearly of no consequence to them.

Third, and perhaps most important of all, if Iraq were to fire SSMs at Israel, especially ones with chemical warheads, it would prove to the entire world that Iraq's disclosure to the UN, in which it claimed that it had no such weapons in its possession, was a bald lie. Launching such missiles could only lead to broader and deeper supervision and harsher sanctions against Iraq. Lastly, even if Iraq still has some launchers, missiles, and chemical warheads, it stands to reason that they are less operationally effective than those she had during the war, having been concealed under dubious conditions for such a long time. In other words, using them today against Israel would subject Iraq to severe retribution without providing much benefit.

Thus Israeli fears of Iraqi missiles and chemical weapons in response to the occasional tests of power between Iraq and the US are exaggerated.

It is therefore highly questionable whether Saddam would repeat the same blunder in similar circumstances. Given that Iraq did not use chemical weapons when it was in prime shape militarily, the likelihood of it doing so in its present, weakened condition, after a crushing defeat, is extremely small. Moreover, such apprehensions in Israel erode Israel's image of strength and, worst of all, they are likely to increase her enemies' self-assurance.

NOTES

1. *Ha'aretz* and *Ma'ariv*, 3 April 1990.
2. *Ma'ariv Report*, p. 26; *Yediot Aharonot*, 27 January 1991 (at that time the Pentagon assumed that Iraq's secret weapon was a Scud with a chemical

warhead); *Ha'aretz*, 27 January 1991, and 3 February 1991.

3. *JDW*, 27 April 1991 and 12 December 1991; The UN Special Commission (UNSCOM) for the Disarmament of Iraq (Iraqi Declaration of Proscribed Materials and Assessment of Iraqi Data Declaration), November 1991.

4. For the impressions of UN inspection teams regarding the slipshod condition of chemical SSMs, cf. D. Albright and Mark Hibbs, 'Iraq's Bomb Blueprints and Artifacts', *Bulletin of the Atomic Scientists*, January–February 1992, p. 36.

5. On the problematic fuses and 'primitiveness' of Iraq's chemical SSMs, cf. Major General Ben-Nun, *Yediot Aharonot*, 1 February 1991; General D. Shomron, 'At best Iraq has a primitive and ineffectual chemical SSM', *Ha'aretz*, 3 February 1991; Head of IDF Intelligence, in *Ha'aretz*, 5 February 1991; and General E. Barak, 'They might have a primitive chemical SSM that can cause limited damage...', *Ha'aretz*, 4 February 1991.

6. Cf. S. Feldman, 'Israeli Deterrence Put to the Test', in *Gulf War – Implications*, p. 174.

7. *Ma'ariv*, 4 February 1991; *Ha'aretz*, 4 February 1991.

8. *Ha'aretz*, 3 April 1990.

9. *Ma'ariv*, 30 December 1990.

10. This analysis is given in the author's paper, 'The Strategic Singularity of the Iraq–Iran War', delivered at the International Conference on the Iraq–Iran War, held at Tel Aviv University, 4–7 September 1988 (hereafter, A. Levran, 'Strategic Singularity'). Also cf. A. Levran, 'The missile threat and chemical weapons', *Ma'ariv*, 14 August 1990.

11. Cf. A. Levran, 'The missile threat and chemical weapons', ibid.; A. Levran, 'Masks May Give Saddam Dangerous Ideas', ibid.; Amiram Cohen, 'An interview with Aharon Levran – The Doomsday Weapon', *Al ha-Mishmar*, 25 January 1991; and A. Levran, 'Projections Should be Realistic', *Jerusalem Post*, 19 September 1990.

12. Quayle's comments are cited in *Yediot Aharonot*, 1 February 1991, and those of the French Chief of the General Staff in *Yediot Aharonot*, 27 January 1991 and *Ha'aretz*, 28 January 1991. The 'confidence' that Saddam would use chemical weapons was also expressed in a report to the British Cabinet stating that Saddam had authorised his commanders in the field to use chemical weapons (*Ha'aretz*, 3 February 1991).

13. A. Levran, 'SSM Memorandum', p. 23.

14. US Secretary of Defense R. Cheney said he 'does not believe an Israeli response would break up the Coalition, in view of statements by Arab Coalition partners who made it clear that there might be an Israeli response if attacks on her continue,' *Ha'aretz*, 5 February 1991.

15. A. Levran, 'Strategic Singularity', ibid.; A. Levran, 'SSM Memorandum', ibid.

16. A. Levran, 'Masks', ibid.; R. Pedahtzur, 'Giving up Deterrence', *Ha'aretz*, 14 October 1990.

5

Israel's Self-restraint and its Deterrence Posture

Israel's self-restraint with regard to Iraq's SSM attacks during the Second Gulf War immediately raises the question of whether, and to what extent, this adversely affected her deterrence posture. This question remains highly relevant, despite the commonly held view among the Israeli public and wide circles abroad that Israeli forbearance in the war was a wise strategic policy.[1] The question must still be discussed, first and foremost, because of the following grave facts:

(a) An extremely sensitive Israeli nerve centre – its civilian population – was repeatedly pounded by missile attacks.

(b) Israel was attacked without having directed any military or political provocation at Iraq prior to the war.

(c) Israel did not punish its Iraqi attackers, nor make any military response against them.

This gives poignancy to the question of Israeli restraint and its implications for its present and future deterrent capability, a cornerstone of Israeli defence doctrine.

FAILURE OF ISRAELI DETERRENCE IN THE WAR

Before trying to grapple with the central issue, we must discuss, if only in brief, the theory of deterrence, especially from the Israeli perspective.[2]

In strategic confrontations between adversaries and hostile

81

states, deterrence is ultimately a reflection of what is worthwhile for each side before resorting to military action. Deterrence generally functions when one of the parties estimates that, despite the temptations or provocations facing him, initiating a war is not worth his while; he decides that he is liable to lose more than he could gain or, to put it simply, that he will be decisively defeated or will have to pay an extremely high price for his actions. The essence of deterrence is to maintain sufficient military power to persuade the enemy to refrain from initiating a war or taking hostile action by conveying the message to him that such action will in no way pay off – that he has reason to fear decisive defeat or at least severe retribution.

Deterrence is not an autonomous, independently variable factor, but rather is symbiotically linked to the ability to win decisively at war. Without the ability to overpower the enemy in battle, or to cause him intolerable expense and suffering, deterrence may not work. It is precisely these abilities that figure centrally in the calculations of cost-effectiveness or reward and retribution regarding a war initiative. Moreover, a negative change in one's battlefield capability – in one's likelihood of winning a war decisively – immediately has an adverse impact on one's deterrence posture.

Although with deterrence one generally presumes a rational analysis of the situation, such an analysis is often accompanied by errors in assessment, such as miscalculating the ratio of forces between adversaries, misreading the overall picture, including the political situation (beyond sheer military prowess), and underestimating the adversary's willingness to pay a heavy price to realise his war aims. Bear in mind that rationality and wisdom do not necessarily go hand in hand.

Hence deterrence is not an absolute strategic asset; rather, it is relative and fluid. As a rule, there is no such thing as the perfect deterrent when dealing with conventional wars, in contrast to non-conventional ones. Apart from physical assets such as military might, deterrence also depends on intangible factors such as national strength, will and determination, the international context, support of allies, existing alternatives, and timing. We may say that deterrence is actually the combination of a number of factors, the central ones being military might, national readiness to use force, and the international background.

This point is very important in view of the shallow contention that, once a war erupted, deterrence never existed from the start. The correct observation is that a deterrence capability existed until war became imminent, ceased to function once war erupted, and, depending on the war's outcome, will either be enhanced or will drastically decline. It is essential to be aware of the relative, fluid nature of deterrence, the ultimate test of which is its ability to prevent a war or, alternatively, to postpone it as long as possible. Where a deterrence capability exists, it can be eroded yet this need not necessarily lead immediately to war, since the decision to initiate a war can have many reasons and causes, of which deterrence, for all its centrality, is but one.

Considering the two dominant factors in the Arab–Israeli conflict – quantitative asymmetry between the parties, on the one hand, and rather deeply rooted Arab hostility towards Israel, on the other – it is surprising that Israeli deterrence could operate at all. In fact, these two factors should have brought about a perpetual situation of active warfare between Israel and the Arabs. The fact that this has not been the case and that there have been substantial intervals between wars indicates that Israeli deterrence basically functions, although, given the overall conditions of the conflict, it is not and cannot be perfect. An outstanding illustration of this is the War of Attrition, which broke out in October 1968, about a year after the greatest Israeli victory – the Six Day War (June 1967). Moreover, the period from 1967 until 1973 (the Yom Kippur War) was one of the shortest intervals between the fully-fledged wars that have been fought between the Arabs and Israel proving how deterrence can be fragile and fluid.

The asymmetry of the parties, mentioned above, is also a basic handicap to Israel's ability to win wars decisively. This is true for several reasons. First, the IDF can win a war against the Arab armies, yet it cannot defeat them in the Clausewitzian sense of enabling Israel to impose its will on the Arabs to bring the conflict to an end. This asymmetry also prevents Israel from being able to eradicate Arab hostility towards it by military means. Israeli military victories do not lend themselves to direct and immediate translation into clear political achievements. Second, the quantitative asymmetry gives the Arabs a much better military absorptive capacity and the ability to hold out longer than Israel, a tiny country that is extremely sensitive to losses, damage, and the other effects of war. Third, the oil factor also plays an important rôle in regional actors' conduct – they feel protected from total defeat due to their possession of such a critical economic asset. They can, therefore, better afford to initiate a war and sustain its dire consequences than can Israel. On the other hand, they cannot defeat Israel, because of its military superiority and ability to defend itself well. It is, therefore, clear that any weakening of Israel's posture as a militarily strong nation – whether absolute, relative, or as a matter of perception – also adversely affects Israel's deterrence posture.

Many of these factors were manifest in the Second Gulf War, in which Israel's conventional deterrent capability essentially did not function against Iraq. Even the deterrence posture of a superpower – the US and the broad Coalition – was totally ineffective against Saddam Hussein, however. In this regard, Saddam made faulty assessments in three areas: first, with respect to the ratio of forces assembled against him; second, with respect to the extent of US and Coalition determination to expel him from Kuwait and to weaken Iraq's military machine so that Iraq would not be able to impose its will on the region; and third, with respect to the outcome of the war that would break out. Nevertheless, the fact that Saddam did not use non-conventional weapons in the Second Gulf War, in spite of his threats, indicates that deterrence did have some weight.

Why was Saddam Hussein not completely deterred? With regard to the US and the Coalition, the answer is that he did not believe that their forces would take action against him, for, as the US Ambassador had told him, 'the American Administration does not take a stand on inter-Arab territorial disputes.'³ Saddam's faulty assessment of the situation might also have been based on the Bush Administration's tolerant policy towards Iraq, disregarding Baghdad's earlier intolerable behaviour and actions (such as its use of chemical weapons and its brutal treatment of the Kurds during the First Gulf War and thereafter). Iraq's presumptions were further buttressed by the Administration's direct and indirect assistance strengthening Iraq with strategic materiel. Saddam Hussein would surely also have kept a close eye on the many heated debates within the US and would have noted the reluctance of American public opinion regarding military intervention on behalf of Kuwait (typified by the rhetorical question – 'Shed blood for a gas station?!').

Moreover, Saddam Hussein may have believed that, should he be mistaken and should force actually be used against him, Iraq could hold its own and the Coalition would crumble, primarily because of the heavy casualties Iraqi forces would inflict on them in ground battles in a protracted war. Presumably Saddam's mistaken assessments were nurtured in no small part by his victory over Iran (in the First Gulf War). The US failures in Vietnam (in the 1970s) and in Lebanon (1982–84) would also have added to Saddam's confidence that he could be a match for the US. In summary, the answer to why Saddam was not deterred by the Coalition rests in the fact that he had grossly misjudged the situation.

As for Israel's failure to deter Saddam, the picture is rather different. Although Saddam presumably did not take Israel's military strength or determination to respond lightly, and notwithstanding his presumed reluctance to open an additional front against himself, it must be assumed that he desired, even needed, a military response or other involvement on the part of Israel. It is also possible that the equivocal outcome of Israel's war in Lebanon (1982) and the great distance between Israel and his own country may have led Saddam to discount Israel's conventional strength somewhat. Be that as it may, a central component of his strategy appears to have been to involve Israel in the war, against its will, in order to dissolve the Coalition, especially its Arab component, and to take the heat off himself. Even before the war it was evident that Saddam had very few active strategic options for responding to the Coalition, should war break out.

Under these circumstances, Israeli deterrence had very little chance from the outset. Saddam Hussein might have assessed that the direct benefit and collateral advantages of drawing Israel into the war would be greater than the price Iraq would have to pay. This was especially the case when a distance of over 1,000 km separating the two parties would grant Iraq's infrastructure and power centres a degree of immunity against the IDF. Perhaps also the price of damage to Iraq's infrastructure or to its SSM deployment in western Iraq was not too dear for Saddam to bear. He would have estimated that Israeli intervention against Iraq would necessarily implicate Israel in a war or major hostilities with Jordan, and perhaps even with Syria. Under these circumstances he probably would have calculated that the Arab states would not be able to remain indifferent to Israel's actions, due to the popular pressure that would be aroused; thus Saddam would disrupt the war that was being fought against Iraq.

There remains the question of why Saddam continued firing missiles at Israel even after he had realised that Israel would not fulfil his expectations and be drawn into war. There are two possible explanations: one, that he still hoped that by continuing to inflict losses and damage on Israel, and by affronting her prestige, his missiles would eventually create a situation in which Israel would not be able to continue its self-restraint; and the other, that his continued missile launchings stemmed from his uncurbed hatred of Israel, the country that had supported his sworn enemy, Iran, in the First Gulf War (the Irangate scam, and so forth), and, above all, had destroyed his prestigious Osirak nuclear reactor in June 1981. When hatred and revenge guide policy decisions, the relative weight of rational considerations decreases; then deterrence becomes less effective.

EXAMINING ISRAELI DETERRENCE POSTURE IN THE
WAKE OF THE WAR

Has Israel's future deterrence posture suffered as a result of her
self-restraint in the Second Gulf War? The answer to this
crucial question is far from simple and can be approached
from two diametrically opposing points of view, each supported
by weighty arguments.

School A: Israeli Deterrence was not Harmed

• All the Arab world knows that Israel had the desire and the
military capability to retaliate against Iraq, but that it was
prevented from doing so due to exceptional circumstances.
These circumstances will not necessarily recur in the future,
especially if Israel faces direct threats from its immediate
neighbouring adversaries. In other words, in the Second
Gulf War Israel did not show forbearance due to its being in
a position of weakness, but rather due to sober considerations and exceptional strategic conditions.

• Others, namely the US and the Coalition forces, were doing
the job for Israel. Under such convenient circumstances,
why should Israel not have shown 'sophisticated' restraint
from which she stood to gain much, namely a favourable
political image, extensive financial assistance from the US
and Germany, and special defence aid, including Patriot
missiles?[4] All this was achieved without Israel actually
investing much. Syrian and Egyptian spokesmen, including
President Mubarak, claimed, 'Look how much Israel has
gained only because of a few fire-works landing in her territory.' Moreover, they added, why should Israel be so unwise
as to intervene and foil the defeat of one of her stronger
enemies?

Two citations are in order here. A Radio Monte Carlo
correspondent reported on a letter President Mubarak sent
President Bush at the beginning of the war, in which the
former expressed his 'concern about the military and economic aid to Israel.'[5] At the time the Syrian foreign minister

called a meeting of Europe's ambassadors to protest to them about their 'growing affinity to Israel.'[6]

• Why should Israel have become involved in military intervention contrary to the better judgement of its good friend and ally – the US – which strongly wished the IDF to stay out of the war? In wars to come, however, the Arabs would have no guarantee whatsoever that American interests would dictate that Israel refrain from striking back at them.

• This war was the first in which American units had rushed to the defence of Israel, and perhaps this attests the sense of obligation and great closeness existing between the two states. It is true that these units were sent to Israel primarily to comfort it psychologically and especially to keep it outside the circle of belligerents; yet this may have established a binding precedent on the part of the only remaining superpower in the foreseeable future to rush to Israel's aid in wars to come. The regional parties, after all, did not fail to note that the US rushed to the aid of Kuwait and Saudi Arabia.

• The Arabs, like others in the Second Gulf War, witnessed what air power and advanced military technology can do even to a militarily strong country such as Iraq; and Israel has had such prowess and capabilities for some time, and is continuously improving them further.

• Punishing an aggressor like Iraq, continuing sanctions against it, and disarming it of dangerous weapons may well serve as a powerful deterrent to any future Arab aggression. Such measures can provide concrete realisation of the high cost and severe damage and humiliation that might be inflicted against a country for what are considered to be acts of aggression. In the final analysis, the cost of aggression in terms of retribution far outweighs its possible rewards.

• The Second Gulf War also brought home to the states of the Middle East that it is difficult, if not impossible, to fight a war of any consequence without the patronage of a superpower, especially when this patron has no opposing superpower. The Arabs and pro-Soviet countries were undoubtedly aware that their traditional patron, the USSR, had, for all intents and purposes, abandoned its active role in the political arena, including the Middle East, leaving them at the mercy of the only remaining superpower, who happened to be the friend of their foe.

- Above all, Israel still maintains a nuclear edge which could be quite crippling to the Arab war option. In the Gulf War this advantage at least deterred Iraq from using chemical weapons and neutralised a key regional power factor in confrontations with Israel.

School B: Israel's Deterrence was Eroded

- Deterrence is bound hand-in-glove with credibility and this involves projecting an image of national strength and determination. Israel certainly lost some of these two assets in the Second Gulf War. After all, Israel's leaders repeatedly informed Saddam in no uncertain terms that if he were to attack the country or its population, Israel would respond immediately in a crushing and decisive manner. Prime Minister Yitzhak Shamir cautioned: 'Anyone who dares attack Israel is likely to bring great calamity on himself.'[7] Defence Minister Moshe Arens cautioned Saddam against attacking Israel, 'since he could expect a hard aerial response.'[8] On another occasion, Shamir stated: 'Those who may be plotting to attack Israel know very well that they will have to pay a truly dreadful price,'[9] as well as: 'If we are attacked, without doubt we shall retaliate, and whoever has attacked us will be very sorry he did so.'[10] Foreign Minister David Levi went so far as to say in an interview, 'Whoever attacks Israel won't live to remember the day.'[11] And Shamir again: 'If Saddam tries to attack or harm Israel, he will be making a terrible mistake and will have to pay a very dear price.'[12] Arens again is quoted as saying 'Saddam knows that if Israel is attacked, it will respond, and how she will!'[13] After the first SSM attack, Chief of the General Staff General Dan Shomron said 'We shall not let this blatantly aggressive behaviour pass without a suitable response.'[14]

Yet none of these numerous, unequivocal warnings were carried out. Of course their purpose was to deter Saddam Hussein and boost Israel's morale, yet failure to act on them clearly detracted from the credibility of Israel's leaders.

- Israel's sensitive home front and innocent civilian population were subjected to repeated missile attacks and submitted to what was surely a trying and extremely embarrassing situation. This had a detrimental impact on the traditional image of Israel's civilian home front as being immune in time of war. This immunity has always been a paramount interest for Israel. Israel's forbearance was equally a blow to its image as a country that responds promptly and forcefully to any strike against its population and vital interests.

- The Arabs saw Israel in distress – many of its inhabitants were on the move from place to place throughout the county, as if panic-stricken – and they could conclude that they had exposed one of Israel's more sensitive weak points. This would make it worthwhile for the regional parties to take greater military risks against Israel in the future in order to hit it again where it is most vulnerable.

- The Arabs hostile to Israel could view the SSM attacks on Israel as having removed a psychological barrier of fear of Israel and as having undermined Israeli defence doctrine, as they had claimed after the Yom Kippur War (1973); this could increase their self-confidence *vis-à-vis* Israel.

- It is true that Arab countries and regional capitals are also vulnerable to Israeli strikes; but Arab leaders have demonstrated less sensitivity to losses and the price of war than Israel due to their greater powers of endurance and their ability to absorb military blows. They need not, therefore, be deterred by Israel lashing out at the corresponding targets –

certainly not now that the major Arab armies are capable of retaliating against Israel with SSMs. Images are especially important in the balance of power and in deterrence. In this sense Israel has certainly been adversely affected, because the asymmetry between the parties in terms of their sensitivity to attack on civilian populations has become much more evident to the Arabs.

- There is no absolute guarantee that the US, especially with an Administration headed by a President with Bush's attitude towards Israel, will rush to the latter's rescue in the future. It stands to reason that the US's affinity and long-standing sense of obligation to Israel will persist; but the US has been shown to be a country whose aid may arrive very late, and influential circles in the US are likely to oppose a costly military engagement. Moreover, in view of cutbacks in the US armed forces, it is doubtful whether they will have sufficient and suitable expeditionary forces to deter regional rulers such as Saddam in the future. Furthermore, the US will not have a base nearby or a friendly neighbouring state in which it can amass forces to rush to Israel's rescue (as Washington did in Saudi Arabia when Iraq invaded Kuwait).

- The Second Gulf War revealed an uncomfortable level of Israeli dependence on the US. This may indicate that in the future the US is not only likely to forsake Israel, but may also compel Israel to refrain from taking military action against regional aggressors in response to severe provocation, or at least to moderate its military response to them.

- As we have said, distributing gas masks and chemical self-protection kits to Israel's population (Israel is the only beleaguered country in the Middle East, in fact in the entire world, to have done so) could be viewed by Israel's enemies as granting legitimacy to new rules of the game, including the possibility of chemical weapons being used against a non-combatant population. This indirectly conveyed the unfortunate message that Israel no longer relies, as it had in the past, solely on her offensive deterrent capability – on preventing war, punishing the enemy and exacting a high price for war.

Choosing between these two schools of thought, and determining what this signifies for the future of Israeli deterrence, is not particularly complicated; yet it is not without its dilemmas. It is not complicated because the test of deterrence, in the final analysis, is whether or not wars break out. Indeed, no war has broken out in the region since the Second Gulf War, nor does one appear to be on the horizon. Some analysts even go so far as to claim that Israeli deterrence has never been so good. As proof of this thesis they cite the peace process, in which the Arabs altered their traditional hardline attitude and sat down to direct bilateral negotiations with Israel. But the minor shift that has occurred in Arab attitudes in the conflict should not necessarily be ascribed solely to the power of Israel's strategic deterrent. This specific change stems more from the Arabs' view of the US, currently the world's only superpower and the country that saved them from a megalomaniac, who could have changed the entire balance of power in the Arab world. More importantly, the perception in the Arab capitals was that the Bush Administration, in contrast to any of its predecessors, would at long last apply heavy pressure to Israel, to reach a settlement closer to Arab preferences. Arab military cooperation with the US during and in the aftermath of the Second Gulf War can only reinforce such an approach.

This is not to say that Israel's deterrence has waned or ceased, but it should not be overestimated or unduly burdened. In addition, one must distinguish between military superiority, which Israel hopefully still retains and which is more of a quantitative physical concept, and deterrence capability, which is a somewhat abstract concept and is certainly more fluid.

It is hard to escape the conclusion that Israel's deterrence posture was somewhat eroded during the Second Gulf War, at least in terms of employing firepower in a war. In the past, the primary risk of war for Israel stemmed from massive Arab ground forces executing a surprise attack, even for limited war aims. Today Israel faces an additional menace, namely missiles launched from afar, with relative ease, against all its sensitive targets.

Moreover, the heavy price that Israel's opponents formerly had to pay for such a surprise attack, namely Israel immediately transferring the battle arena to their own territory with large sections being physically conquered or destroyed, could now be avoided by attacking Israel using distant firepower alone. In the event of such a war, perhaps Israel will not rush, as it had in the past, to carry the fighting quickly into the enemy's territory solely because missiles are fired at its territory. Regional parties could therefore resort to a war model in which firepower dominates at the expense of troop manoeuvres on the ground. Even if this scenario does not take place and there is no war at all (although Israel should win even in a war where firepower and SSMs are the dominant factor), this does not preclude the possibility of such perceptions prevailing among regional decision makers, and in this respect it constitutes an intrinsic erosion of Israel's deterrence posture.

Questions of deterrence in the wake of the Second Gulf War should also be examined in the context of the cumulative results of the Arab–Israeli wars. It is not difficult to discern that since the Six Day War (1967), Israel's military victories have been characterised by a 'descending victory curve'. Although Israel achieved a brilliant tactical, operational land victory in the Yom Kippur War (1973), it is well known that strategic victory was not achieved. The Lebanese War (1982) also conveyed ambiguous messages: on the one hand, Israel won a striking victory against the Syrian air force and part of its SAM disposition (on which many Arab armies had been relying heavily); yet on the other hand, the IDF ground operations and movements were clumsy and some operational goals were not achieved or were critically delayed. Later, during the IDF's three-year stay in Lebanon, it became evident that there had been difficulties coping with terrorism and guerrilla warfare conducted by a hostile local population. Israel was also hampered by the lack of political consensus at home and its inherent weaknesses such as oversensitivity to casualties, and an inadequate ability to cope with prolonged war efforts. Similarly, the way Israel has been coping with the Palestinian *Intifada* and terror in Judea, Samaria, and Gaza has also not contributed to the IDF's overall deterrence capability. Thus the IDF's diminishing military successes over the past two decades perhaps do not attest complete erosion of her deterrence capability (which, as we have noted, is *ipso facto* relative and fluid), but nor do they enhance it.

Notwithstanding the above, Israel apparently still preserves military superiority over regional opponents and their armed forces. This supremacy pertains largely to the quality of Israel's air force and its overall technological edge, notably its sophisticated weapons systems. Hopefully it also pertains to two other pillars of military proficiency – high quality manpower and skilled command echelons, and, of equal importance, high combat motivation. The expression of this superiority lies, first of all, in the IDF's ability to prevent an aggressor from achieving his war aims, as well as in the ability to punish him militarily or make him pay dearly. These proficiencies and capabilities seem sufficient to preserve Israel's deterrence posture for the coming years, notwithstanding the erosion it may have suffered in the Second Gulf War, if not earlier.

Israel is in no way militarily omnipotent, as Israelis and foreigners often tend to portray it, be this to serve their political ends ('since Israel is so strong, it can afford to make territorial concessions to the Arabs'), or because they simply overestimate her strength. The Second Gulf War undoubtedly brought some of Israel's hidden but existing weaknesses to light. The major lesson for Israel is clear, if unpleasant: if, under certain circumstances, an Arab ruler should wish to achieve a specific vital aim, even at the high price of starting a war, then Israel's deterrent will not necessarily function.

NOTES

1. We shall not dwell on this specific point in this study. Note, however, General Ben-Nun's comments to *Ma'ariv*, 19 June 1992 and to *Tzevet*, July 1992, justifying Israeli restraint on the grounds that if it had intervened it would have been blamed for Saddam Hussein remaining in power. Of course this cannot be a central or persuasive argument for or against Israeli restraint in the war.

2. This is also discussed, although from different angles, by S. Feldman, 'Israeli Deterrence Put to the Test', and by E. Inbar and S. Sandler, 'Israel's Deterrence Strategy Revisited', *Security Studies*, Winter 1993–94.

3. This follows from the report on his conversation with US Ambassador to Baghdad, Ms April Gillespie, on 25 July 1990. Cf. J. Hoagland, 'Transcript Shows Muted US Response to Threat by Saddam in Late July', *Washington Post*, 13 September 1990. Also see *Ma'ariv Report*, p. 17; S. Gazit, 'The Mystery of the Interview with Ambassador Gillespie', in *Gulf War – Implications*, p. 31; and Gillespie's testimony in the Senate after the war, cited in *Davar*, 21 March 1991. Similarly, from the conversation with G. Wilson, then *chargé d'affaires* at the American Embassy in Baghdad, on 6 August 1990, 'Saddam could have been led to believe that the US would even accept him as the regional policeman of the Gulf.' Cf. A. Baram, 'Israeli Deterrence, Iraqi Responses', *Orbis*, Summer 1992.

4. The reference is to the Administration's consent to the initiative taken by Congress in 1990 to provide Israel with excess army materiel in the sum of $700 million, as well as its later authorisation of special economic aid totalling $650 million, as compensation for Israel's damages in the war. Cf. *International Herald Tribune*, 7 March 1991.

5. Cited in *Ha'aretz*, 28 January 1991. In addition, two major Egyptian newspapers wrote revealing editorials on the subject. *Al-Akhbar*: 'Israel wins without firing a shot. While Iraq is being pummelled, Israel is reaping political, military, and financial benefits, thanks to her atypical policy of self-restraint. No one has brought more benefit to Israel than Saddam Hussein. The missiles saved Israel from the mire of 1982 [the Lebanon War – A. L.] and in ten days transformed her from an aggressor to a victim.' *Al-Joumhouriya*: 'With relatively slight losses to her population, Israel can permit herself to sit with hands folded and watch from the sidelines how her mighty enemy, Iraq, is being destroyed; and in addition, she enjoys a new and respectable international image.'

6. Cited in *Ha'aretz*, 30 January 1991. In addition, the Syrian newspaper *Tishrin* launched a vigorous attack on Western aid to Israel, and Israel's Minister of Foreign Affairs at the time, David Levi, expressed concern regarding President Assad's complaints about Patriot missiles being sent and deployed in Israel.

7. *Davar*, 10 August 1990.

8. *Ma'ariv*, 16 August 1990.

9. *Ha'aretz*, 23 August 1990.

10. *Ma'ariv*, 31 August 1990.
11. *Jerusalem Post*, 27 September 1990.
12. *Ma'ariv*, 5 October 1990.
13. Cited in *Ha'aretz*, 25 December 1990.
14. *IDF Daily Press Release*, 18 January 1991.

6

Diminished Risk of War Despite Persistent Military Build-up

Although deterrence has a direct and strong bearing on the risk of war, it is only one among a number of factors causing, or preventing, the outbreak of such a conflict, so the overall danger of an Arab–Israeli war in the wake of the Second Gulf War merits separate discussion. The basic claim here is that, notwithstanding the possible erosion in Israeli deterrence in the wake of the Second Gulf War, the danger of an Arab–Israeli war in the foreseeable future has decreased significantly. Indeed, one of Israel's most important strategic accomplishments in the Second Gulf War, overshadowing most other accomplishments, was that it significantly reduced the risk of war. This is true despite the acceleration in the regional military build-up of SSMs and other qualitative weaponry in the wake of this war (as we shall see below). Having said that, it is still risky to forecast events, especially with respect to the possibility of war, in the Middle East. Our war predictions should be confined to the foreseeable future. To illustrate the difficulty in forecasting Middle Eastern wars it is worthwhile mentioning that, in the summer of 1988 when the long and bloody war between Iraq and Iran had just come to a close, a mere two years later Saddam Hussein would pre-cipitate a serious crisis in the region and involve the world in another fully-fledged war?

From Israel's point of view, the risk of war in the past decade, as well as in the foreseeable future, can be attributed to two potential developments: establishment of an 'eastern front', or Syria initiating a war on its own. Both of these deserve our attention.

DIMINISHED RISK OF WAR

The emergence of an 'eastern front' consisting of Syria, Jordan, Iraq and Saudi Arabia has always posed a substantial military dilemma for Israel due to the problem of the IDF having to fight against a number of enemies on several fronts simultaneously. In such a situation a sequential approach (not fighting all the foes at the same time but in succession) could ease the burden on the IDF, but it would not solve other dilemmas facing Israel. Not the least of these difficulties is that Israel would be faced with a race against time, for a protracted war jeopardises the likelihood of an Israeli military victory being clearly manifest on the battlefield.

The hard military blow that the US and the Coalition forces landed on the infrastructure and armed forces of Iraq has made it difficult for this country to play a central rôle in an eastern Arab military alliance against Israel in the foreseeable future. Previously, Iraq had always played a key rôle in an 'eastern front' due to its ability to contribute a considerable ground and air ORBAT. Prior to the last war, it was estimated that Iraq could contribute eight to ten divisions, some 200 fighter planes, and a similar number of fighter helicopters to a war initiative. Such an Iraqi expeditionary force was almost as large as the entire Syrian army and twice the size of the Jordanian and Saudi Arabian armies combined. An expeditionary force of such magnitude would have made combat more difficult for the IDF by aggravating the balance of forces.

In the wake of the Second Gulf War, Iraq was markedly weakened militarily, especially in terms of the major and 'special' pillars of its force: weapons of mass destruction, and the means of their delivery, namely SSMs and aircraft. Nevertheless, Iraq still retains substantial military might – approximately half of its ground formations and air units.

Moreover, it has certainly hidden an unknown quantity of SSM launchers and missiles, as well as other non-conventional weapons. Her ground forces today have been decimated, and number some 350,000 soldiers (compared to approximately a million before the war), some 30–40 divisions (in contrast to some 60 before the war), and some 3,000 tanks (as opposed to about 6,000 previously); yet its army also rid itself of 20–30 poor quality, second class infantry divisions.[1] Today, the backbone of Iraq's army consists of some ten armoured and mechanised divisions, five divisions of the Republican Guard (compared to seven before the war), and several groups of special forces.[2]

Although the Iraqi army has reorganised and has largely been rehabilitated after the war, one must remember that it suffered a severe beating and considerable demoralisation and trauma during the war, from which it could hardly recover with ease. It is also doubtful whether large portions of this army will be capable of playing a central part in combat in the foreseeable future, especially 1,000 km from home. An Iraqi expeditionary force fighting at such a distance would need considerable defensive cover and air support, but a large part of Iraq's qualitative air ORBAT was destroyed or transferred to Iran during the war (the Iraqis naïvely thinking that Iran would provide a safe haven). In terms of numbers, the Iraqi air force remains quite strong – some 380 fighter planes, and some 500 fighter helicopters – but in terms of quality, many of its aircraft are not considered first class.[3] More importantly, the supply of essential spare parts and the operational fitness of this force after the war are highly questionable.

Furthermore, post-war Iraq will undoubtedly be more suspicious of its immediate neighbours – Iran, Turkey and Saudi Arabia. Baghdad will long remember what these countries, especially the former two, did to her in the war. It will be dangerous for Saddam's régime to lead an adventurous policy far from her borders, involving large, qualitative portions of its forces, without fearing that Iran and Turkey might take advantage of the situation to devour parts of its territory. These and similar apprehensions are likely to persist even if there is a future reconciliation between Iraq and its neighbours. Iraq's ability to achieve comprehensive reconstruction after the war depends to a large extent on its strategic-political position – on whether the international sanctions against Iraq continue and whether the UN efforts to locate and destroy all the non-conventional components and ballistic missiles persist. The longer these endeavours continue and the more comprehensive and successful they are, the more Iraq's military might will be curtailed.[4] We can rest fairly well assured that Iraq will find it difficult to initiate or play a central role in an 'eastern front', contributing a substantial expeditionary force. The personal hostility between Saddam Hussein and Syrian President Assad might also make it quite difficult to establish a successful war coalition in the foreseeable future.

Syria is the other major war menace for Israel. However Damascus, long advocating the need for 'strategic parity' with Israel, will not rush to confront the IDF in war without the participation of other Arab armies as well, including an Iraqi expeditionary force. Syria will not do so because President Assad is a more enlightened ruler than Saddam Hussein. He is known to be ruthless (he slaughtered tens of thousands of Syrian Moslem zealots in the city of al-Hama in 1982), and harbours deep-seated hostility towards Israel, evident in hundreds of his speeches, despite his recent change of tone. His present change in tactics regarding Israel is due to his lack of any other viable political choice. Be that as it may, many years of ruling (since 1970) have made President Assad, unlike Saddam Hussein, a sober, cautious and calculating ruler. Syria, therefore, will not rush to war for fear of being defeated or suffering a severe blow if it stands alone against Israel.

Moreover, Hafez Assad is a shrewd strategist and is certainly aware of the many advantages of his present change in policy. Joining the Coalition against his foe, Saddam Hussein, has already yielded political fruits for Syria. First, he has complete control over Lebanon. President Assad had been at an impasse in the quagmire of Lebanon since 1975, but as soon as he joined the Coalition against Iraq in the summer of 1990 he received a green light from the American Administration, and in October 1990 he succeeded in storming the Presidential Palace in Beirut and ousted General Aoun (the then Lebanese head of state). Second, in the wake of the Second Gulf War, Syria received about $3 billion from Saudi Arabia and the Gulf States for its co-operative behaviour in the war – a considerable sum to aid Syria's tottering economy. Third, by moderating its traditional ideological extremism, Syria reduced its political isolation in the region and in the international community. This isolation had weighed heavily on Syria; so much so that, by December 1989, President Assad finally broke the taboo instituted in the wake of the Camp David Accords (1979), and renewed relations with Egypt (even though he had promised not to do so as long as the flag of Israel still waved in Cairo). Joining the Coalition helped Hafez Assad change the extremist image of his régime in the world at large and at the same time weakened his sworn enemy, Saddam Hussein.

Lastly, for the first time in many years the question of the Golan Heights (which Syria lost as a result of its aggression in June 1967) has been placed seriously on the political agenda. This points to Assad's possible desire and intention to follow in the late President Sadat's footsteps and to replace the military option pursued until now by political struggle.

Equally, the military lessons that Syria might learn from the Second Gulf War are unlikely to make it eager to become involved in a military conflict against Israel in the near future. Syria witnessed the poor performance of the Iraqi armed forces,[5] which were equipped with very similar weapons to Syria's own.

The Syrians seemed to be highly impressed by the triumphant performance of the Coalition's air force and qualitative weaponry. It is obvious to them that only Israel can repeat such triumphs, although (in their opinion) at the cost of much higher casualties. They also observed the ease with which the Coalition's forces penetrated the Iraqi fortifications and defence lines built in Kuwait, although they are aware of the differences and the strength of their own fortified deployment in the Golan Heights. The Syrians also witnessed what happened to Iraqi armour (such as tanks and personnel carriers) when pitted against smart and stand-off air and land weapons, as well as what happened to the Iraqi air defences, which were very similar to their own. Syria's rulers also saw the impact that SSMs had on the Israeli home front; but presumably they realise that such missiles cannot decide the outcome of a war and certainly cannot conquer or win back territory.

As we have mentioned, President Assad was also worried by Israel's accumulation of Patriot missiles, which, as ATBMs, could, he felt, neutralise the SSM threat. Moreover, the Syrians are also aware of their own lack of strategic depth, with the IDF positioned only about 50 km from their capital, Damascus. Hence, despite the recent, impressive Syrian military build-up following the war, it is quite unlikely that Damascus would risk a military option single-handedly in the near future.

Furthermore, even if Hafez Assad wished to pursue a military option, he would find it extremely difficult because his superpower patron, the USSR, has disappeared from the arena. In fact, Soviet support of Syria began to wane when President Gorbachev told Assad in Moscow, in April 1987, that there was no military solution to the conflict with Israel. Subsequently, difficulties and delays began in the delivery of Soviet arms, which Syria had, until then, been receiving either free of charge or at considerably reduced prices. By then it became clear to President Assad that he could no longer count on full Soviet support and material backing for his policies. This, in particular, and his political isolation in general, prompted him, *inter alia*, to renew relations with Egypt in 1989. Thus, having perceived his country's political distress, and apparently having no other viable option, Assad began to gradually tone down Syria's radical posture on the international scene, including the conflict with Israel.

President Assad can no longer totally ignore the policy and

wishes of the US, as he has in the past, because America has rehabilitated its weak image since the period of the Vietnam war and since its unsuccessful intervention in Lebanon in 1983–84. More importantly, as far as Assad is concerned, is the fact that, in the Second Gulf War, the US demonstrated its ability and determination to come to the aid of its friends, Kuwait and Saudi Arabia. Hence Assad may realise the danger that, if Israel were to be attacked, here too, the US might rush to the aid of its ally. The warm relations that have developed between the Clinton Administration and Israel in recent years, can also be a significant constraint on Damascus fostering war with Israel. These superpower configurations undoubtedly have a moderating effect on the Syrian potential war option, especially since the political alternative has begun to appear more promising.

Some analysts still believe that Syria has the option of seizing the Golan Heights, or parts thereof, by means of a 'land grab' – a sudden and limited onslaught – or by a war of attrition. But these are less likely scenarios, since Israel could seize the opportunity to expand the scope of battle to a fully-fledged war, in which Syria would be likely to find itself alone, especially without the patronage of a superpower. There is also no guarantee that Syria would be able to attain significant strategic objectives from such a limited war; the military outcome may actually be to its total disadvantage. It is important to note that Syria has not resorted to a military option, including attrition, since 1973. We can thus say that it would be quite risky for Syria, on its own, to engage in a war against Israel in the near future and it is important that the Syrian leadership should be aware of this.

These considerations should be borne in mind when considering talk in Israel and abroad about the Arabs possibly going to war if there is no positive movement in the political process – specifically, if they are not given the territory lost in the Six Day War or if the Palestinians are not granted full political satisfaction. Yet, if we analyse the situation rationally (and although the atmosphere in the area occasionally becomes verbally heated, on the whole local leaders have been pursuing reasonable policies), it is difficult to see the Arab states, especially the principal ones concerned – Syria, Egypt and Jordan – going to war for the Palestinian cause and thereby jeopardising their own régimes and vital interests. This central argument appears to hold notwithstanding the Arab rhetoric on the Palestinian issue and the territories.

Even the question of the Golan Heights, a tiny area (approximately 1,100 square km) in comparison to all of Syria (approximately 185,000 square km), is not as important to Syria as the Suez Canal, formerly under Israeli control, had been for Egypt. Aside from concerns of ideology and prestige (the idea that 'Arab land' must be regained, as Egypt retrieved Sinai), the Golan Heights do not appear to be of pressing interest to Syria. Certainly, the fact that the IDF on the Golan Heights is positioned relatively close to Damascus makes Syria uncomfortable; but it has addressed the situation by setting up multi-layered depth defences consisting of several lines of fortifications – which protect Damascus quite well – and by substantially increasing the size of its forces, thus allowing greater breathing space.

It appears that Syria can live with the burden of not regaining the Golan Heights for many more years. If this were not the case, Syria's leaders would have acted with far greater urgency in their many rounds of negotiations with Israel.

Syria is also opposed to an independent Palestinian state in the area which it views as 'Southern Syria', notwithstanding pronouncements that it is not prepared to accept return of the Golan Heights without an overall solution to the Arab–Israeli conflict (including a solution to such issues as 'Arab land', and 'rights').

Jordan, troubled by its military and strategic weakness, will similarly not rush into a military adventure for fear that a war would destroy its infrastructure and centres of power. Jordan has little reason to jeopardise its present integrity, security and well-being for territories from which it had disengaged formally since the summer of 1988. Jordan is still licking its wounds from the mistake of siding with Saddam Hussein, a trauma which is bound to make the country much more cautious in future major policy decisions. Furthermore, King Hussein seems to be committed to the October 1994 peace treaty with Israel.

In the Second Gulf War, Saddam Hussein proved the deep cynicism of the Arab states with respect to the Palestinian problem: his patronage of the Palestinians was merely a cover for his ugly ambitions, and once he had been defeated, he was quick to drop his patronage. We may conclude that the vital interests of the major Arab countries and their rulers override any pan-Arab or Palestinian concerns.

Notwithstanding the above, a qualifying remark is in order. One must not forget that the Middle East can be subject to sudden upheavals stemming from the mistaken assessments of its rulers or from possible changes of régime. Unfortunately, in this region we have political entities that stand on shaky foundations and that view genuine democracy, liberalism and pluralism as alien concepts. Moreover, the present autocratic rulers also happen to be threatened by the Islamic funda-mentalism that is becoming more entrenched in large parts of the region. Therefore, despite the seemingly smaller risk of war today, and notwithstanding the political process being led by the US, it is not clear yet that there has been no genuine revolutionary change in the Arabs' perceptions and attitudes with regard to accepting Israel's enduring existence in the Middle East. So latent military dangers still exist, although they remain a long way from imminent or foreseeable war against Israel.

REGIONAL MILITARY BUILD-UP IN THE WAKE OF THE WAR

The systematic military build-up among the states in the region after the war is one of the obvious indications that no fundamental change has occurred in their attitudes towards Israel. The 'New World Order',[6] which connotes, among other things, restraint in arms proliferation and abjuring the use of force to solve conflicts, has not had much impact on the states in the region, including Syria and Iran, nor on quasi-moderates like Saudi Arabia and Egypt. This build-up also stems from regional rivalries that do not directly concern Israel, although the Arab–Israeli conflict is still central, certainly for the states surrounding Israel. The current military build-up is a direct result of the Second Gulf War, and is potentially menacing in the long term. It certainly has an impact on the regional balance of power, on the prospects of settling the conflict, and on programmes for curbing proliferation of non-conventional weapons systems, as well as conventional arms control.

Moreover, the true intentions and positions of a state are generally better revealed by its efforts to build up military strength than by its verbal moderation. This build-up is what really threatens Israel in the long run. Although the process of regional military escalation in the wake of the Second Gulf War does not disprove the view that the risk of war in the region in the foreseeable future has substantially decreased, it is nevertheless important to survey the more prominent attempts at build-up by several Arab and Moslem states.

SYRIA: INDEFATIGABLE EFFORTS TOWARDS A MILITARY BUILD-UP

Even before the Second Gulf War was over, Syria's Minister of Defence Mustafa T'las hurried to Moscow to purchase several dozen more modern fighter planes – Mig-29s and Sukhoi-24s – and some 700 T-72 tanks and 300 self-propelled guns from other sources. He may also have shown keen interest in Sukhoi-27 aircraft and SA-10 missile batteries[7] (the Russian equivalent of the US Patriot). Syria's purchase of dozens of Scud C surface-to-surface missiles from North Korea, along with their production technology, should be viewed as especially grave. Occasional indications pointed to the fact that Damascus may also have taken action on the purchase of M-9 missiles from China, and may have acquired the knowledge to produce them locally.[8]

The SSM deals were concluded prior to the Second Gulf

War, but their delivery was accelerated in the wake of the war. The range of these two types of missiles (500 and 600 km, respectively) will give the Syrians better coverage of any military target within Israel while making it more difficult for the IDF to cope with them (namely, to eliminate or neutralise them) once they have been deployed deep in Syrian territory. Such a situation will encumber execution of the IDF's offensive option against the missiles and may enhance Syria's own confidence in her SSM capability. From the outset this capability was meant to counter-balance Israel's air advantage over Syria. Of greater concern is the Syrian purchase of the missiles' production technology, because this enables the country to circumvent restrictions on the proliferation of ballistic SSMs, and, more importantly, to extend the range of the missiles (as Iraq did), or even to develop more advanced warheads.[9] In any event, the Syrian army has added a fourth brigade of SSMs to its ORBAT (in addition to the Scud B, SS-27 and Frog brigades). Syria is expected to begin full production of its Scud C missiles in the second half of 1996.

Syria's recent arms acquisitions add considerably to its military strength, which is already quite impressive, both in terms of armed forces and conventional weaponry, as well as providing a certain non-conventional capability. The Syrian army has at its disposal 11 armoured or mechanised divisions, (one was established after the war), in which there are some 4,900 tanks (including recent acquisitions from Russia and the Czech Republic).[10] This gives Syria a similar number of divisions, and twice the number of tanks as Egypt, a country four-and-a-half times bigger than Syria in terms of population. Note that after the US reduces its ORBAT to nine divisions (or fewer), Syria will have more divisions than the US. To be fully aware of Syria's ground strength two points must be added: (a) all Syrian divisions consist of four brigades (rather than the normal three) and (b) besides the 11 armoured and mechanised divisions, the land ORBAT also consists of another 11 independent brigades.

Aside from Scud Cs and perhaps also M-9s, Syria has several hundred Scud B missiles, a large number of which are equipped with operational chemical warheads. Syria also has chemical air bombs (it is probable that Syria's Frog missiles also have chemical warheads), and more than once has tested some nerve-gas bombs.[11] Syria's capabilities in chemical weaponry are noteworthy and are far more menacing to Israel than Iraq's. Syria has also begun to indicate an interest in the nuclear domain, and seems to have concluded the purchase of a small – 80 kilowatt – research reactor from the People's Republic of China.[12] This conventional and non-conventional military build-up will enable Syria to narrow the quality gap between its armed forces and the IDF while also giving it a relatively greater offensive capability. It is noteworthy that Syria's arms acquisitions were made possible by her receipt of large sums of money (approximately $3 billion) from Saudi Arabia and the Gulf States as a reward for its participation in the Coalition against Saddam Hussein. But it preferred to divert these resources to purchasing arms, rather than using them to build up its failing economy (as if the Second Gulf War did not also have any moderating political message). Syria is indebted by some $11 billion to Russia (half of it for earlier weapons acquisitions) but there is little chance that Damascus will repay it and this is causing Moscow to avoid concluding the 1992 and 1994 arms deals with Syria. In any event, Syria's massive and diverse military build-up was probably intended not only as a deterrent to Israel, but perhaps also as an inauspicious indication of her intentions for the more distant future.

The Syrian efforts at military build-up, which accelerated in the wake of the Second Gulf War, apparently stem from their lessons from this war: first, that old weapons need to be replaced with qualitative arms and munitions; second, that Syrian leaders still feel a lack of 'strategic parity' with Israel, which they perceive as having a similar military-technological edge to that of the US; third, that the political struggle needs to be fought from a position of strength, while keeping open other options for the distant future. In any event, in quantity and quality the steady Syrian build-up is not necessarily consonant with 'peaceful, conciliatory' intentions nor with

Assad's utterances about a 'peace of the brave'. In the final analysis, one must pay closer attention to Syria's actual development of its military capabilities than to its words of moderation, which could be masking other intentions and possibilities.

SAUDI ARABIA: AMBITIOUS MILITARY BUILD-UP

This country, extremely apprehensive about its fate before the war, came through with a sense of self-assuredness and highly ambitious plans for a military build-up. The Saudis' own self-confidence grew because, for the first time in their history, their ground and air forces fought in a fully-fledged war and acquired combat experience.[13] Their pilots even downed Iraqi planes in the Coalition's aerial campaign against Iraq. On land, they fought side by side with major Coalition forces and commanded all the Arab expeditionary units in the war.

The greatest cause of concern for Israel, however, ought to be Saudi Arabia's grand plans for a military build-up, both qualitative and quantitative, which began to be implemented when the Kuwait crisis was in full swing in the summer of 1990. As soon as the crisis broke out, US President Bush approved the transfer of a large quantity of arms to the Saudis (24 F-15 C/D planes, 150 M-60-A3 tanks, hundreds of Stinger AA missiles, and thousands of low-uranium anti-tank shells). Shortly thereafter the Administration announced its intention to sell Saudi Arabia arms on a vast scale involving some $23 billion.[14] For political reasons this transaction was divided into two stages. The first, totalling $7.3 billion and including six Patriot anti-aircraft batteries, 12 Apache fighter helicopters, 150 modern M1-A2 Abrams tanks, 200 modern Bradley APCs (armoured personnel carriers) and additional weapons systems, was immediately approved by Congress.[15] The second stage, totalling some $15 billion, was postponed at the time, but is being implemented piecemeal[16] and will presumably include 235 modern M1-A2 major battle tanks, 36 Apache helicopters, 72 advanced F-15 fighter planes, and 20 Patriot batteries.

The ambitiousness of this acquisition programme does not lie in the large quantity of weapons; Saudi Arabia has always purchased large quantities of modern weapons systems from the US, Britain and France. The startling element lies more in Saudi intentions to more than double the size of its military force to some 200,000 soldiers (compared to approximately 80,000 soldiers in 1991), as Prince Khaled ben-Sultan, the Saudi commander of the Arab forces in the war, announced in April 1991. Saudi Arabia plans to reach a ground ORBAT of seven or eight divisions. This far-reaching intention has not been fulfilled as at early 1996 and the Saudi army is still based on brigade level. However, it grew from 14 brigades in 1991 to 17 brigades today (armoured, mechanised infantry, and para-troopers) and some 20 independent battalions (mostly infantry). Likewise, the Saudi army is in the process of reno-vating and absorbing its weaponry – especially tanks and armoured personnel carriers. It appears that, until the Second Gulf War, the Saudis concentrated primarily on building up their air power due to their great fear of Iran, but lately they have been shifting the emphasis to strengthening the ground component of their armed forces. Even after the Second Gulf War the Saudis have not ignored the air component and, as we have mentioned, they purchased 72 F-15PX planes – a similar version to the F-15E – from the US, bringing their total (including 24 F15s-C/D) to 96 today). One should bear in mind that the F-15E is considered to be the most advanced aircraft in the world, having both interception and attack capabilities. It is interesting that President Bush approved the sale 'in order to prevent unemployment' in the US and thus promptly neutralised all opposition to the deal. By early 1996 Saudi Arabia already had 150 fighter planes of very high qual-ity at its disposal, which is more than any other Arab state and is similar to the quantity possessed by Israel. Another 120 high-quality planes are due to be delivered in the next few years. In any event, Saudi Arabia owns more F-15s than Israel, and, with its recent purchase of an additional 72 planes, the number of F-15s the Saudis will own in the future is expected to exceed 160.

The Saudi military build-up would not be a problem for Israel were it not for doubt about the Saudis' ability to defend themselves adequately. Three basic factors give the Saudis problems in self-defence: (a) the vast territory to be defended – an area of some 2.5 million square km; (b) the existence of especially sensitive targets – oil and holy places; and (c) the Saudis' lack of manpower in general, and of suitable personnel with the necessary expertise to serve in the armed forces, in particular, which consequently makes them have to depend on foreign military manpower including technicians and advisers.[17] It is highly doubtful whether Saudi Arabia will be capable of defending itself on its own against future aggression by radical and dangerous neighbours (particularly Iran and Iraq). It is also not beyond the realms of possibility that one day the arsenal of extremely modern weapons that Saudi Arabia is acquiring might fall into the hands of one of these countries, or into the hands of extremists who might take over within Saudi Arabia itself. As far as Israel is concerned, the Saudi build-up has other direct implications, such as the possibility of a Saudi expeditionary force with modern arms participating in an 'eastern front' (as happened in the past), and/or transferring some of these arms to other Arab states in time of war.

The problems of Saudi military build-up are well known to its American patron. Indeed, the US is interested in new security arrangements in the Gulf area. The US wishes not only to increase arms sales to states in the region but also to maintain a greater and more permanent military presence there. Specifically, the US seeks to maintain a strong naval force in the Persian Gulf, to deploy several air combat squadrons in bases in Saudi Arabia and some of the Gulf states, and to station weapons and military provisions in emergency reserve stores there. However, apart from maintaining a standing naval force in the Persian Gulf and stationing several combat squadrons in Saudi Arabia and elsewhere in the region, thus far the US has encountered opposition, primarily against it setting up emergency reserve stores for its ground forces.[18] On the other hand, other Gulf states, with

111

Kuwait, Bahrain and Oman in the lead, have been more forthcoming and have even signed defence agreements and consented to joint military exercises.[19]

These developments convey a double message to Israel. On the one hand, it seems that the Saudis are becoming politically more moderate, as they move closer to the US and the West for fear of their radical neighbours. On the other hand, Israel also perceives a significant military menace in the very existence of much-advanced weaponry in Saudi Arabia. These arms are particularly likely to be used directly against Israel in the event of radical political upheavals in Saudi Arabia and the surrounding area.

From a strategic-political standpoint, close US–Saudi relations and US–Gulf States relations might detract from the importance of the strategic co-operation between the US and Israel and might cool the special intimacy between the two. It is no wonder that those circles in the US that clamour to weaken ties with Israel point to the fact that the latter did not participate in the war against Iraq (as if Israel did not wish to) and assert that Washington could rely on its Arab friends alone.

IRAN: THE DANGER OF FUNDAMENTALISM AND OF REGIONAL DOMINATION

Iran is one of the major beneficiaries of the Second Gulf War, due primarily to the weakening of its traditional enemy, Iraq. Saddam Hussein's blunder in transferring 148 of his planes (including 115 high quality fighter planes) there during the war is simply another Iranian war gain. It was quite clear to Iran's leaders that they should hasten to take advantage of the war's results to restore their regional dominance, which suffered considerably from the débâcle in the First Gulf War. It is also obvious to them that their armed units, which were practically non-existent as a viable military force in the First Gulf War, must be made more professional and qualitatively rehabilitated. This is essential because Iraq's military power was not totally demolished in the Second Gulf War. The US victory and its increased presence in the Persian Gulf is another grave source of concern to Iran, also causing it to accelerate its military build-up.

Iranian efforts at military reconstruction began by the end of the First Gulf War, and have continued energetically in the wake of the Second Gulf War. These efforts included sizeable arms purchases from the USSR/Russia, North Korea, China, and elsewhere. Acquisitions from Russia included, *inter alia*, some 60 highly advanced aircraft (including Mig-29s and Sukhoi-24s) and approximately 500 T-72 tanks together with the technology for producing them. They also purchased three submarines. Most of these deals have already progressed quite far in terms of deliveries and implementation.[20] In the years after its war with Iraq Iran could have spent tens of billions of dollars on defence.[21] Even if these sums pertain to overall defence expenditures and not solely to military procurements, they appear rather excessive.[22] Either way, we are dealing with an annual figure approaching Iran's annual defence expenditure during its war with Iraq (estimated then at $6–10 billion per annum). Iran has been able to finance this increased defence expenditure due to its improved ability to produce oil in large quantities in comparison with the war years, although, all in all, its present economic condition is still not particularly good.

These trends certainly give cause for concern. As at 1996, Iran possesses some 200 advanced combat aircraft (including the Iraqi planes that defected during the war) whereas, in the First Gulf War, it had practically no air force at all. Moreover, for the first time in its history, Iran has fighter planes at its disposal (such as Sukhoi-24s) that can reach and directly hit Israel, as well as other combat aircraft that can be incorporated into, or reinforce, the Syrian air force.[23] With the additional tanks that it has purchased, Iran will have over 1,000 tanks – still a much smaller armoured fleet than the Iraqi or Syrian ORBAT, and of limited significance in ground operations, especially over long distances. Nevertheless, these developments coupled with the increase in the number of ground divisions (from 28 in 1991 to 40 in 1996) represent gradual yet steady progress, giving Iran a good chance of again becoming a major regional power, as in the days of the Shah. Iran's increased self-confidence after the Second Gulf War finds expression in its aerial attack, in early April 1992, on the Mujahedin who were taking refuge inside Iraq, some 80 km from Baghdad and in its forceful takeover of islands in the Persian Gulf in the same year.

Of greatest concern to Israel, however, are Iran's efforts to obtain long-range SSMs and non-conventional weapons, including nuclear weapons. Its acquisition of submarines is also worrying, although not directly from Israel's point of view, since the submarines' purpose is to improve Iran's naval capabilities, especially against the US fleet in the Persian Gulf and the Straits of Hormuz, and also, primarily, to enable Iran to exert its power over the region. Iran's seizure of the Abu Musa Islands in the southern part of the Persian Gulf, in late August 1992, should be seen in this context. Iran has great potential for causing instability in the Persian Gulf and the Middle East. Iran is one of the three countries in the region (the other two being Iraq and Israel) with the greatest awareness of the menace of SSMs. In fact it was the first country in the region, indeed in the world, since the Second World War, to make strategic use of such missiles. In 1985, it began to fire Scud Bs at Baghdad in retaliation for the Iraqi air force's repeated bombing of its infrastructure and population centres. Iraq's counter-attacks on Teheran and other cities towards the end of the First Gulf War, using some 200 al-Hussein missiles, made a deep impression on Iran's leaders. This explains Iran's current extensive efforts to expand its SSM capability, and its close co-operation with North Korea and China come as no surprise.

Iran has already purchased many dozens of Scud C missiles from North Korea along with their production technology. Their 500 km range is not sufficient to reach Israel, but it certainly represents a significant threat in the theatre of the Persian Gulf. Moreover, Iran might try to increase, even double, the range of these missiles. The Iranians are also directing efforts at indigenous development of the Tondar-68 missile, a version of one of the Chinese M-missiles designed to reach 1,000 km or more.[24] More significantly, it is almost certain that Iran seems to have acquired North Korean 1,200 km range No-Dong-1 missiles, currently in the final stages of development. It is quite possible that Iran is even assisting North Korea in the missile's development, financially as well as operationally. It has been reported that Teheran even assists by ground testing the missile in Iranian deserts (as the North Koreans find difficulty in executing long-range tests in and around their country). These missiles will, for the first time, place Iran in a position, technologically, of being able to make a direct strike at Israel.

Iran's aspirations to develop nuclear weapons are of deep concern both to Israel and to the West. This nuclear aspiration dates back to the time of the Shah, but was temporarily abandoned by the leaders of the Khomeini revolution; however, the latter changed their position once they learned of Iraq's ambitious nuclear programme and the steady work on its development. Such aspirations, after all, accord with Iran's traditional notion of being the regional power. Yet, unlike Iraq, Iran appears to be progressing in its nuclear programme relatively slowly and cautiously. Iran, like Iraq, is approaching nuclear military development along a broad front, by enriching uranium and producing plutonium indigenously. The Iranian nuclear project receives assistance from a variety of places, including China, Pakistan, India and Argentina. In August 1995 the Iranians enlisted the assistance of Russia to resume the building of two nuclear reactors at Busheer on the Persian Gulf.[25] In addition, persistent, although as yet unverified, reports claim that Iran has even managed to obtain several nuclear bombs that allegedly disappeared from a Soviet base in Kazakhstan. Russia and Kazakhstan vociferously deny this, and the entire episode is shrouded in mystery. Yet some consolation can be found in the fact that the Iranians, reputedly, 'will find it hard to decipher the nuclear code'.[26]

It is worth mentioning that Iran's nuclear endeavours are

motivated not only by hegemonic ambitions, but also by its desire to deter the US. After all, the US easily defeated Iraq, and the increased American military presence in the Gulf poses a permanent obstacle to Teheran's regional aspirations. Consequently, even if Iran does not possess operational nuclear weapons today, it is feared that she might acquire them within five to ten years if it develops them indigenously and uninterruptedly, or sooner if it receives significant aid from outside sources.[27] While increasing its military build-up, Iran has been conducting a foreign policy designed to project a more moderate image. It appears to be taking a more pragmatic approach in its foreign policy towards the states of the Saudi peninsula as well as towards the West. However, its steady acquisition of modern, qualitative weaponry and its military build-up into a major regional power, in the wake of the Second Gulf War, leave little doubt as to its true intentions.

Iran's strategic priorities probably concern Iraq and the Persian Gulf, yet additional, more far-reaching, options remain in its hands. Moreover, Iran's deep-seated hostility towards Israel, its avowed opposition to the 'peace process', its continued subversiveness and full support of the terrorist activity of Hizballah fundamentalists in Lebanon and of Palestinian organisations such as Hamas and the Islamic Jihad, its involvement in the Islamic republics of the former USSR, its deployment of units of the Revolutionary Guard in Sudan, and its involvement in the subversive activity of Islamic fundamentalists in Egypt, Turkey, Algeria and else-where all attest to the grave menace which a fundamentalist Iranian state poses to Israel and to the whole region. Most of all, Iran symbolises the new threats facing Israel from a circle of more distant states in the wake of the Second Gulf War.

ATTEMPTS BY LIBYA AND OTHER ARAB STATES TO BUILD UP DANGEROUS ARSENALS

Libya's military build-up is not necessarily related to the Second Gulf War, although presumably the lessons of the war have not been lost on it. Its present build-up is a continuation of its endeavours from before the Second Gulf War. The problem, here, is not so much Libya's conventional forces but its declared intention to develop non-conventional weapons and ballistic SSMs.

The danger in Libya's huge arsenal of conventional weapons lies primarily in the possibility that they could be transferred to the states surrounding Israel as a backup in case of war, thus upsetting the military balance for Israel and adversely affecting the IDF's ability to determine the outcome of armed confrontation. Libya's attempts to obtain ballistic SSMs and non-conventional capabilities might even affect Israel directly. Fortunately, Libya's efforts in these domains have not thus far proved successful.

In the chemical field, the story of Libya's fraudulent actions concerning the facility at Rabta has not been forgotten. It appears that, since this was uncovered, the Libyans have begun building a new, subterranean chemical facility at Sabkha, south of Tripoli, again allegedly with Western assistance.[28]

Their efforts in the field of nuclear weapons have been continuing without much success.[29] Nevertheless, for some time now Libya has been working at developing a 1,000 km range SSM, which could pose a direct threat to Israel and to southern Europe. However, Libya has encountered some difficulties in development and has fallen behind schedule.[30] Meanwhile, it appears that North Korea has also offered to sell to Libya the 1,000–1,200 km range No-Dong-1 missile that it has developed, along with information to enable Libya to produce it locally.[31] Libya may even be helping to finance development of North Korea's No-Dong-1 SSM.

Thus far we have reviewed worrying military build-ups in four countries in the region, besides Iraq. Other Arab countries, including Egypt and Kuwait, have not been lagging behind in this regard. The Second Gulf War has impelled them to accelerate the pace of their military build-up, especially with qualitative weaponry, such as air platforms, PGMs, and stand-off munitions. One of these countries –

Egypt – also seems inclined to renew efforts to develop non-conventional capabilities, yet the emphasis in Egyptian conventional build-up is on the most advanced aircraft (F-16 C/D), the Abrams M-1A1 tank (including licensing for indigenous production), and arms and munitions that serve as force multipliers – stand-off munitions such as gliding bombs, Maverick air-to-surface missiles, night-vision combat systems, Apache helicopters, and more.[32] It is interesting to note that despite the peace treaty with Israel, Egypt is still maintaining the vast size of its armed forces and is extensively modernising its weaponry with advanced Western systems. This is particularly true with regard to its air force which now primarily consists of US F-16 aircraft. Likewise, the backbone of its fleet of tanks is composed of American M1-A1, M60-A3 tanks. These tanks and others are integrated into Egypt's 12 divisions (as before 1991), 11 of which are armoured and mechanised.

ISRAEL'S MODERATE BUILD-UP

Israel, meanwhile, has not been ignoring the regional military build-up, nor has it been indifferent to the lessons of the war with respect to technology and qualitative weaponry; however, budgetary limitations hamper her from competing adequately. The IDF has actually decreased its ORBAT and has cut back its active weapons.[33] Nevertheless, the IDF should be strengthened by the special Congressional appropriation of 1990, transferring US army surplus in the sum of $700 million to Israel. Israel's 1994 decision to purchase F-15I fighter planes was a most important weapon procurement as it was designed to allow the IAF to deliver a large payload of munitions at ranges of over 1,610 km. Likewise, the IAF has acquired some more Apache attack helicopters, which performed well in the Second Gulf War. In addition, the armoured formations were enriched with Merkava II and III tanks, now constituting the backbone of its tank fleet. Israel has also been working hard on the Arrow

(ATBM) project in co-operation with the US, and the US has been financing the greater part of this. Presumably Israel's primary interest lies in continued indigenous development and procurement of smart munitions and PGMs. The Second Gulf War demonstrated the need for such weaponry and reinforced the emphasis which the IDF places on it. The possibility of special advanced technology being transferred from the US to Israel is also high on the agenda, as always, awaiting Washington's final approval. All of this may help counterbalance the serious military build-up in the wake of the Second Gulf War and maintain Israel's military edge.

To conclude, although the risk of war against Israel in the foreseeable future has decreased significantly, there has been no radical change in the situation as far as long-term potential military menaces are concerned. The threats have assumed another form, and in the wake of the Second Gulf War have perhaps even increased in certain respects, due to the build-up in conventional and non-conventional arms, and due to the increased threat to Israel on the part of distant Moslem and Arab states. Even today, therefore, Israel must invest more in national security in order to counter possible unexpected developments in the region, such as the Second Gulf War, especially since impressive military development cannot be accomplished overnight, but is, rather, a process which spans many years. This is, however, no simple matter due to Israel's economic limitations, and its social and other needs. Nevertheless, Israel must not find itself helpless in the face of new potential threats that are steadily seething beneath the surface in the wake of the Second Gulf War.

NOTES

1. In this regard, the remark made by former Iraqi Defence Minister General al-Majid to Baghdad's *Al-Thawra* newspaper, in January 1992, is instructive: 'The government decided to build a small, but powerful, well-maintained and effective army. We have turned a page in determining the size of the army.' Cited by Edward B. Atkeson in 'The Middle East: A Dynamic Military Net Assessment for the 1990s', *The Washington Quarterly*, Spring 1993.
2. An interview with the Commander of the IAF, *IAF Journal*, October 1991;

interview with Moshe Arens, *Bamahane*, 4 December 1991; *JDW*, 25 April 1992; CIA Director Robert Gates, in a speech to the Nixon Library Conference, 12 March 1992 (published in *USIS*, 16 March 1992, hereafter 'Gates' Speech'); quote from a speech by Israel's Chief of the General Staff, cited in *Ma'ariv*, 10 November 1991; A. Cordesman, *The Military Balance in the Middle East 1991*, November 1991.

3. As we mentioned in Chapter 2, note 9, the Iraqi Foreign Minister admitted that 148 planes had been flown to Iran, 115 of them fighter planes, including 75 Sukhoi aircraft (24 of them Sukhoi-24s!), 24 Mirage-F1s, and 16 Migs (including Mig-29s!), as reported in *Ma'ariv*, 14 April 1991. American intelligence estimates refer to 137 aircraft being transferred to Iran, including the types mentioned above, as well as Adnan 1 (IL-76) air control and warning aircraft. Cf. *JDW*, 6 and 27 April 1991.

4. Thus far the UN has made many dozens of inspections and destruction missions, in which they have identified and begun to destroy tens of thousands of chemical bombs and artillery shells, have destroyed equipment for manufacturing SSMs and some 150 missiles of all sorts, and have exposed and destroyed a considerable part of Iraq's nuclear programme. By mid-July alone, such inspections numbered over 50. Cf. 'Existing Non-Proliferation Effort', White House Fact Sheet, *USIS*, 14 July 1992.

5. Syria could have learned mixed lessons from the Second Gulf War: it might have been impressed by Iraq's defiant stand against the Coalition's forces but it seems that, deep down, Syria's leaders, especially Assad, are cognisant of the strategic lessons that, in the final analysis, are far from flattering to Iraq.

6. For an authoritative explanation of the term 'New World Order' by the person who coined this phrase, see the Introduction by President Bush to the pamphlet, 'National Security Strategy of the US,' The White House, August 1991.

7. On the Syrian build-up in general, cf. Chief of IDF Intelligence, in *Bamahane*, 10 June 1992, and 23 October 1991; speech by Israel's Chief of the General Staff, *Ma'ariv*, 10 December 1991; Commander of the IAF, in *IAF Journal*, October 1991. On the possibility of some of the deals not being realised due to difficulties in financing them, cf. *IAF Journal*, February 1992. Also, the *Middle East Military Balance 1994–95*, (Jaffee Center for Strategic Studies, Tel-Aviv University 1988).

8. *JDW*, 7 December 1991; *Ma'ariv*, 1 June 1992.

9. *Ma'ariv*, 1 and 15 June 1992, and 9 July 1992; *Davar*, 9 July 1992; *Congressional Record Service*, 19 November 1991.

10. *Davar* and *Ma'ariv*, 9 July 1992. Also the *Middle East Military Balance 1994–95*, ibid.

11. *Ha'aretz*, 16 June 1992; speech by Israel's Chief of the General Staff, ibid., 'Gates' Speech', ibid.; also cf. L. Spector, 'Nuclear Proliferation in the Middle East', ibid. For Syria's and Egypt's chemical weapons programme, see D. Shoharm, *Chemical Weapons in Egypt and Syria*, (BESA Center for Strategic Studies, Bar-Han University, June 1995).

12. Speech by Israel's Chief of the General Staff, ibid.; 'Gates' Speech', ibid.; L. Spector, 'Nuclear Proliferation in the Middle East', ibid.

13. *Ha'aretz*, 3 February 1991.
14. *Washington Post*, 29 August 1990; on the Saudi build-up, cf. D. Gold, 'The Gulf Crisis and US–Israel Relations', in *Gulf War – Implications*, p. 75; A. Cordesman, ibid.; and the speech by the Chief of the General Staff, *Ma'ariv*, 10 December 1991. See also the *Middle East Military Balance 1994–95*, ibid.
15. *New York Times*, 5 January 1991; D. Gold, ibid.; *JDW*, 16 November 1991, 14 December 1991, 1 February 1992, 7 March 1992, 28 March 1991; and ACDA, February 1992.
16. *JDW*, 16 November 1991, 7 March 1992, and 28 March 1992.
17. Recently there have been indications that even the Saudis are having difficulty financing their arms acquisitions. They are still paying off the huge cost of the Second Gulf War, and their overall current expenses are quite large.
18. *JDW*, 2 November 1991, and 28 March 1992; *Ma'ariv*, 1 June 1992 (citing an article in the *Washington Post*).
19. *JDW*, 14 December 1991.
20. *Defence Electronics*, March 1992; *Ma'ariv*, 8, 13 and 14 January 1992; *Bamahane*, 20 May 1992; and Y. Bodansky, 'Iran Acquires Nuclear Weapons', *Defence and Foreign Affairs*, February 1992.
21. According to *JDW*, 1 February 1991, Iranian defence expenditures in 1991 were $19 billion, and for 1992 were $14.5 billion. Another report cites $12 billion spent on defence, $4 billion of which are for arms purchases from the Commonwealth of Independent States, *Bamahane*, 1 July 1992.
22. According to a more reliable report, it appears that, in 1991, Iran only purchased $1.9 billion worth of arms; cf. *Ma'ariv*, 23 July 1992, citing a report by the Congressional Research Service, published in Washington. Nevertheless, other reports insist on a figure of tens of billions of dollars for defence and procurements.
23. IAF Commander, *Ma'ariv*, 15 January 1992; *Ma'ariv*, 13 January 1992; IAF Head of Intelligence Research Branch, *Bamahane*, 11 December 1991.
24. *JDW*, 1 February 1992; on Iranian SSMs see also *JDW*, 7 December 1991; *Bamahane*, 20 May 1992; *Ma'ariv*, 1 and 15 June 1992; *Davar*, 7 July 1992.
25. *Sunday Times*, 27 August 1995.
26. *Yediot Aharonot*, 15 June 1992; *Ma'ariv*, 1 May 1992, citing the *European* of 30 April 1992. For a good account of Iran's nuclear effort see D. Albright, 'An Iranian Bomb?', *The Bulletin of the Atomic Scientists*, July/August 1995.
27. See the statement of US Secretary of Defense, William Perry, *Ha'aretz*, 6 January 1995.
28. *Ma'ariv*, 7 and 25 March 1996.
29. Cf. L. Spector, 'Nuclear Proliferation in the Middle East', ibid.
30. Head of IDF Intelligence, *Ma'ariv*, 9 June 1992.
31. *Yediot Aharonot*, 15 June 1992, citing a *Newsweek* survey.
32. ACDA, February 1992; *JDW*, 14 December 1991; speech by Israel's Chief of the General Staff, *Ma'ariv*, 10 December 1991. The *Middle East Military Balance 1994–95*, (Jaffee Center for Strategic Studies, Tel Aviv University, 1988).
33. Speech by the Chief of the General Staff, ibid.

7

Implications of the Second Gulf War for Israel's Defence Doctrine

Although the repercussions of the Second Gulf War for Israel have been discussed throughout this study, this chapter is devoted to highlighting the implications of this war for Israeli defence doctrine. It is appropriate to conclude this study by focusing on Israel's theory of defence, to see how important lessons learned from the war can or should be weighed and integrated.

During the years following the war, various ideas on defence lessons were voiced in Israel from time to time, but it is doubtful whether a methodical analysis or comprehensive and systematic formulation of these notions was set forth – or, at least, none reached learned observers. The reason for this could be that this war was rather exceptional in two salient parameters: it was a unique occasion marked by gross inequality in the ratio of forces (a broad Coalition headed by a superpower versus an isolated, medium-sized, Third World state), and, as far as Israel was concerned, the war was confined to SSM fire on the home front while Israel was prevented from reacting. Hence one might argue that the war does not provide a fully applicable, or relevant, model for armed conflict between Israel and its immediate neighbours, in which altogether different circumstances would pertain.

Another explanation, of a more subjective and psychological nature, can, however, be offered for the paucity of public discussion of the war in Israel. Perhaps there is a subconscious desire among the Israeli people to suppress this war in their consciousness and to view it as an embarrassing, but isolated, episode. Perhaps there is also a feeling, which is far from well-founded, that the region is marching forward towards *genuine peace* so why agonise over unpleasant events of the past?[1]

The Second Gulf War, however, was not simply a fleeting episode in the history of the region, but was rather, as we have pointed out, a traumatic event and an important watershed, both militarily and politically. We cannot, therefore, shirk our duty to thoroughly examine the implications of this war for Israeli defence theory and doctrine.

The Second Gulf War, we believe, is highly relevant to Israeli defence doctrine in six areas; the first three are a direct outgrowth of the war, and the latter three follow from the war's implications. First is the SSM threat, which cannot be regarded as an isolated episode but is likely to increase in the future. In this context one should take into account the general, ever-changing military dangers, present and future, as well as the optimal ways of coping with them. Second is the issue of intelligence, especially early warning, which is particularly important for Israel and its existence in view of its small dimensions, both in terms of population and territory. Third is the role and function of IDF air power in a future war, especially in the light of intriguing remarks on this subject made by IAF commanders after the Second Gulf War.

The lessons of the Second Gulf War also extend to broader areas of defence concepts and doctrine. Thus the fourth area concerns the menace of non-conventional weapons. Chemical weapons were not used in the Second Gulf War, but persistent efforts are being made by countries in the region to obtain mass-destruction weapons systems and the risk of regional nuclear proliferation appears greater than ever.

The fifth area concerns the importance of territory and strategic depth, especially in view of the pre-Second Gulf War claim that the value of these assets has diminished in the *era of the surface-to-surface missile*. The importance of strategic depth must also be examined in the light of the strategic surprise in the outbreak of the Kuwait crisis.

Lastly, to address the issue of a *war of choice* or preventative

124

war is in order. Although the advisability of such a war appears to have declined in the wake of the Lebanese War (1982), nevertheless the experience of the Second Gulf War seems to provide new justification for such an approach.

THE SSM THREAT AND BROADER THREATS TO SECURITY; POSSIBLE RESPONSES

The SSM launchings against Israel in the Second Gulf War, and the future SSM menace to Israel, raise at least two questions of principle. First, should ballistic missile fire be viewed simply as a nuisance, or as a significant strategic threat? Second, if it poses a substantial threat, then what options exist for coping with this danger?

With respect to the first question, it is interesting that, even after the war, some high-ranking IDF circles maintain that aircraft, capable of carrying several times as much ordnance as missiles, still pose the greater menace. A similar view holds that SSMs are primarily psychological, terroristic weapons and are not a threat to survival; therefore, given Israel's limited manpower and materiel resources, it should not involve itself in needless expenditure to meet such a low-level danger.

Serious shortcomings were evident in this approach even before the war, and certainly after it. The Arab and Moslem air forces in the region, for all their menace, do not pose a critical threat to Israel due to the IAF's great superiority. However, even if the potential threat to Israel's survival lies in a massive ground onslaught and not in SSM fire, Israel cannot sit back idly and let its own cities and its civilian population be exposed to recurrent strikes by its immediate or more distant neighbours, whenever they feel like attacking or whenever they happen to become embroiled in other local conflicts. Essentially, SSM launchings are neither a negligible threat nor simply a nuisance to Israel's security.

It is important, therefore, to dwell on what doctrine, and which methods, Israel should adopt to cope with SSMs. Some

IDF circles today still see maintaining an offensive, deterrent capability, primarily in air power, as the principal, if not the only, answer to the SSM challenge. The advocates of this approach view such a capability as versatile and multi-dimensional, since air power is inherently flexible and capable of confronting other, even more perilous, threats too.

Even if we conjecture that the IAF could have been more successful than the Coalition air force in coping with the Iraqi SSMs launched in the Second Gulf War, we cannot be sure that it would have been able to neutralise the threat completely and rapidly, since it is probable that no air force is capable of doing so alone. The IAF would probably have been handicapped by the geographical setting and would surely have had difficulty operating, especially if the Iraqi air force and air defences had remained intact and had not first been put out of action by a third party. Moreover, Israel's air power cannot be fully effective, or at least cannot provide the sole, systematic response, when SSMs are launched from more distant countries, such as Iran, Libya and Saudi Arabia. If missiles in the region are equipped with non-conventional warheads, it is doubtful whether the IAF should be entrusted with the task of confronting them on its own. More importantly, there is no guarantee that the IAF will have sufficient ORBAT in a fully-fledged war to cope simultaneously with SSMs and other military exigencies; and this unfortunately means that the SSM threat will inevitably not receive top priority. In addition, there is always the lingering fear of bad weather impeding aerial operations, notwithstanding the existence of all-weather aircraft. Interestingly, even in this era of technological advances, air forces still bow to adverse weather conditions.

Therefore, even though its resources are limited, Israel must adopt another central option, in parallel, in its security doctrine, namely *active defence*. Anti-missile missiles or other suitable means must be a central component of Israel's defence, no less important than the classical component of offensive air power, in order to cope with the growing threat of SSMs, especially those that might be launched by distant states. Neutralising SSMs in the air by missiles or similar devices will make it clear to the enemy that his launchings are to no avail and that he cannot expect a victory through such fire power alone. Likewise, whoever relies on SSMs as a long-range means of attacking Israel will feel less secure on his home front once that means of attacking is neutralised, and equally important, when he knows that he will be exposed to the mercy of the IAF's depth attacks on his strategic assets. In the Lebanese War (1982), when the IAF was strikingly successful against the Syrian SAM batteries, the Syrians refrained from launching SSMs at Israel, despite their earlier insinuations because the Syrians had been thrown off balance and felt insecure about a key pillar of their military power.

Active defence will inevitably have to be adopted, since the Gulf War showed that Israel's offensive deterrence capability was not viable against Iraq's conventional SSM threat. Although the circumstances of this war were indeed unique, there is no guarantee that they will not recur. Relying solely on offensive deterrence is inadequate as an option for national security in general and against the SSM threat in particular. Furthermore, Israeli air deterrence is likely to be far less powerful against distant countries like Iran and Libya. Recall how Iran suffered eight hard years of war, including countless Iraqi aerial attacks on its cities and infrastructure; yet this neither deterred Iran from continuing the war, nor did it leave a particularly deep impression on its leaders. How, then, could the IDF and its air force deter such a country, operating from a distance of some 1,500 km, or systematically attack it and influence its behaviour?

Simply because the IDF adopts the additional dimension of active defence, this is no reason to fear that it might change its fully justified, traditional offensive posture; rather, it is a matter of suiting the response to the major military challenges existing at present and to those anticipated in the future. Moreover, the IDF's offensive posture on the operational level and its principle of rapidly transferring the battle to enemy soil will always be preserved against the more grave threat (albeit a more distant one today) of a surprise Arab ground offensive.

It should be observed that extensive offensive methods, even if justified, will not be so welcome to world public opinion in the foreseeable future. This shouldn't be an over-riding obstacle to Israel's self-defence yet it constitutes a significant constraint.

Will the most suitable countermeasure of active defence be the Arrow missile system, or the Super Patriot (Pac-3), or a combination of the two, or perhaps some other system developed in the US in the context of GPALS and SDI (if Israel has a chance of purchasing such sophisticated devices)? This question is important technologically, professionally and financially, but it is secondary in terms of doctrinal principles, which clearly call for the adoption of active defence.

The Arrow system, with its relatively high price, has been criticised vehemently, particularly in IAF circles from whom it might obviously divert financial resources. They have not only criticised its underlying conceptual approach (defence as opposed to offence), but have also claimed that it will essentially wipe out Israel's defence budget.[2] Rebuttals to these arguments are found throughout this book. Here we wish to add that investing several billion dollars over a number of years is neither beyond Israel's financial means nor beyond its call of duty, especially when essential weaponry for countering an intolerable threat is at issue. Furthermore, were it not for the Arrow, Israel would surely have to purchase some alternative anti-ballistic system, not necessarily an offensive deterrent, since it cannot leave the central strategic challenge of the day – SSMs and firepower from afar – unanswered. Another counter-argument is that any other alternatives will not be much cheaper, let alone the fact that other systems have not yet been developed or proven.

As for the argument challenging the advisability of fighting cheap arms with expensive ones, two points are in order. First, regional SSMs are not as inexpensive as we have been led to believe. The Iraqis had to pay several hundred thousand dollars for each original Scud missile, and generally had to sacrifice three Scuds to produce two converted long-range al-Husseins capable of striking Israel. It is known that the Saudis paid the Chinese as much as several million dollars apiece for their numerous surface-to-surface missiles. Conventional enhancements of the warheads (such as decoys and cluster configurations), not to mention non-conventional warheads (chemical or nuclear), will raise the price far more. Second, as we noted in Chapter 1, the decisive factor is not how expensive the countermeasures are, but rather the cost of the potential harm that SSMs could do to Israel. Carrying this argument *ad absurdum*, one could envision a situation in which one of Israel's enemies obtains a nuclear bomb as a gift; in such a case would anyone bring up the enormous cost of offensive or protective countermeasures.

Critics often compare the Arrow system with the Lavi aircraft – a project which Israel ultimately abandoned – to illustrate what happens when Israel, a small country, becomes involved in a project that is too big. But these two projects have little resemblance. First, the scope of Israel's acquisition and deployment of the Arrow system can always be adapted and reduced if it becomes unaffordable. Second, at present, total investment in research and development for the Arrow is around $480 million, of which only about $120 million are from Israel's own budget. This may be compared with an estimated cost of $2.5 billion for the Lavi, half of which was actually paid. Third, while research and development for the Lavi was financed by US foreign aid to Israel, the Arrow is being financed exceptionally from the SDI budget, above and beyond regular US aid to Israel. Fourth, Israel–US co-operation in the research and development work on the Arrow programme is strategically invaluable. There was no such co-operation in development of the Lavi (grudgingly supported by the US Administration), nor did that aircraft contribute significantly to US needs. By contrast, Israel's innovative technological contribution in missile interception will be beneficial to the US (and its allies) – a fact that is bound to strengthen the ties and strategic co-operation between the two countries. Israel's deterrence posture benefits in particular from Israel being one of the few countries chosen by the US for joint work on such a technologically advanced project. Fifth, research and development on the Arrow will also help Israel's technological advancement in areas other than missile interception and will benefit its economy by providing employment for technologically-skilled manpower at home, thus keeping such skilled individuals from seeking work on alien shores. The latter point also applied to the Lavi. The difference, however, was that there were many alternatives to the Lavi (such as the F-15, F-16, and F-18), whereas thus far there is almost no alternative to the technology being developed for the Arrow – hence the great importance of assuring the success of this project. After all, it is not for naught that the US is willing to invest several hundred million dollars in the Arrow above and beyond its regular aid to Israel.

Parallel to the Arrow system, another potential method to cope with SSMs seems to exist. SSMs seem to be most vulnerable at their initial boost stage. If they could be hit at this stage from the air by, for example, remote piloted vehicles (RPVs) hovering over suspected launching pads, the danger from SSMs could be drastically reduced. Yet such a countermeasure to SSMs isn't so simple in terms of systematic operation over long distances, intelligence information-gathering and early warning, etc. In any event, such a response, offensive by nature, isn't at all sheer fantasy and might pose in due time a viable competitor to the Arrow and current developments of active defence.

The SSM threat against Israel in the wake of the Second Gulf War also raises the issue of general dangers to Israel's security. While, at present, the immediate risks of the Arabs going to war against Israel have significantly diminished, the potential threat that still seethes beneath the surface, due to a continuing regional military build-up prompted by the lessons of the war and by other factors, has not diminished over the intermediate or long term, especially not in the realm of firepower. From the point of view of Arab and other countries in the region, SSMs and firepower apparently rank quite high as weapons against Israel – even higher than ground troop assaults. Concentrating on firepower and missile-launching enables the Arabs to obtain the utmost advantage from their military skills, which, in the domain of ground manoeuvre, are limited from the outset, and at the same time it helps them to offset Israel's general military supremacy. It is easier to strike at Israel by means of firepower than by resorting to ground troop campaigns. This is especially true when the Arabs can absorb casualties and retaliatory fire better. Moreover, Israel's enemies could expect to receive some superpower backing and a more pro-Arab international atmosphere in a more limited war. As we have mentioned, the threat to Israel of SSMs and firepower from neighbouring states is compounded today by similar menaces from more distant states in the region that, in the past, only risked sending expeditionary forces against Israel. It is, therefore, obvious that the scope and nature of the general military threat to Israel's security, especially in firepower terms, has broadened substantially.

How does this affect Israeli defence doctrine? First, it has become essential to provide military responses of a somewhat different nature from the ones supplied in the past, both in terms of offensive deterrence (not only by means of air power), as well as active defence. Israel must broaden its horizons in thinking about security and must develop means of striking across greater distances. These might consume a large portion of Israel's resources, yet it is hard to see how Israel can manage without them.

Whoever maintains that the spread of the military threat or the change in its nature calls primarily for a political response is begging the question and is even jeopardising Israel's security. Progress in settling the conflict does not depend solely on Israel; rather, as in the past, it depends primarily on a revolutionary and genuine change in Arab attitudes to the conflict. Such a change is unlikely to occur unless the Arabs revolutionise their political and societal culture and genuinely adopt *Western values* such as pluralism, liberalism and democracy. One must also bear in mind that Israel's principal potential adversaries in the region face dangers and threats that do not necessarily involve Israel, and that their military build-up is prompted by other local factors. It seems likely, therefore, that the Arabs will not wish, nor will they be prepared, to accept a political solution with Israel that would weaken their position *vis-à-vis* these other challenges to their security.

In addition, the existence of good military responses to the new threats will only help make the Arabs realise that, in the final analysis, there is little to be gained from resorting to the military option against Israel. This, incidentally, was precisely the case in the global confrontation in which the East finally realised that it could not effectively confront the West. Hopefully this will be the case in the Arab–Israeli conflict. Likewise, effective military responses will enhance Israel's deterrence posture.

While active defence, air power, and special weaponry are central factors in responding to the threat of SSMs and distant firepower against Israel, *smart* weapons systems (PGMs and stand-off munitions) provide an appropriate, even the optimal, response to the threats of the battlefield of the future. No great effort is needed to convince Israel of this, nor does the IDF have much to learn or apply in this field, at least in principle. The IDF has been one of the world leaders in the field since the Yom Kippur War (1973). Israel also demonstrated marked success in its use of PGMs and stand-off munitions in the Lebanese War (1982), especially in the air. It has long been clear to the IDF that advanced technology and qualitative weapons will be the key factors in future full-scale military confrontations. The same goes for electronic weapons, which proved highly effective both in Israel's wars and in the Second Gulf War.

If, on the macro-strategic level, Israel has little to learn technologically from the Second Gulf War, this does not mean that on the tactical-professional level of operating smart munitions it has nothing to learn. Moreover, if there is a military power factor that might be crucial in a future war, it lies in the domain of smart weaponry. Here, perhaps more than elsewhere, the qualitative advantage of Israel over its adversaries, stemming from the Israeli genius and its advanced and progressive society, can and must find expression.

The obvious conclusion is that Israel must enable the IDF to continue promoting its development projects to the best of its ability, notwithstanding economic difficulties and limited resources. This investment will bring a double return in any confrontation that might occur, by reducing losses (Israel's hypersensitivity to losses in manpower and essential equipment is well known) and by contributing to a swift and decisive victory.

Precision-guided long-range munitions also have unique potential for increasing Israel's deterrence by making the military option even less viable for her enemies. Such weapons and munitions will probably make deterrence more credible than ever before for the following three reasons. First, the opponent will sense more keenly that his vital objectives might be far more easily destroyed in a large-scale armed conflict. Second, stand-off and smart ordnance can circumvent or overcome strong ground aerial defence dispositions and reduce human losses, and these factors are critical to Israel in battle (especially when its adversaries count on it so much). Third, such munitions are generally more effective than former means at destroying deeply buried and hardened military targets. This deters the IDF's adversaries from counting on keeping their military assets intact. It will also always prove cheaper to make a large investment in smart defence today than to pay the horrible price of possible failure and heavy damage in a war tomorrow. In sum, such sophisticated weapons have the potential to prevent a full-scale Arab–Israeli war.

ON INTELLIGENCE AND EARLY WARNING

The severe and almost inevitable strategic surprise in the outbreak of the Kuwait crisis proves once more that much greater weight must be given to a properly functioning intelligence system. The absence of good intelligence (in terms of information gathering and processing) during and after the war, including Saddam Hussein's continued deception of UN inspection teams and his far from complete compliance with UN Resolution 687 and others, certainly has an important bearing on the extent of the threat against Israel (and other countries) that still emanates from Iraq.

The problem of Israeli intelligence in the Second Gulf War centred more on difficulty in gathering information than in analysing and assessing it, even though most failures of Israeli intelligence in the past stemmed precisely from misassessments (most notably its failure in 1973). It is well known that the more information is available, the better assessments can be produced, despite the parallel increase in collateral noise. However, the greater the variety and the higher the quality of these intelligence-gathering tools, the better are the chances of obtaining good, reliable and timely information. Nevertheless, all this in itself does not suffice; a good intelligence network must strive to process and distribute information to the appropriate users at all echelons in real time.

During the Second Gulf War, Israeli intelligence, like its counterparts in the West, suffered in the realm of information gathering due to objective factors, although one cannot speak of a blatant intelligence failure here. Israel's intelligence research department strove to cover for the lack of sufficient real-time data by providing more alarmist assessments regarding Iraq. Such an approach is often taken because of a lack of a viable alternative, but it is not a sound prescription for good intelligence, nor is it feasible in every setting.

Worst-case assessments due to insufficient information, or to other causes not based on data, have an inherent risk. In the first week of the Yom Kippur War, for example, Israeli intelligence was asked to provide a worst case assessment in the event of Jordan actively joining in the war. But this request was turned down and intelligence refused to supply such an abstract assessment due to a lack of valid information. This was the case, although the temptation to comply was great, especially in view of the surprise at the war's beginning and the fact that the route to the capital was not very strongly defended and Jerusalem might have been at stake. Such an extreme assessment could have led immediately to a drastic reallocation of Israeli forces on various fronts. Specifically, it could have reduced the forces fighting Syria and Egypt in order to reinforce those in the Jordanian sector; but ultimately this could have been fateful for the outcome of the war, adversely affecting the course of battle in the Sinai and the Golan Heights.[3]

As far as intelligence is concerned, the solution must focus on extending the apparatus for intelligence-gathering mechanisms to states far from Israel, and also on intensifying intelligence operations in nearby states. As mentioned, this is not easy for a small country with scant material and human resources; but, in contrast to the past, it is no longer merely a question of priorities, since, as pointed out, the risks from distant states have become much more tangible, and the alternatives of having insufficient information, or of being dependent on others for attaining it, are not acceptable options.

A key solution for Israeli intelligence is a reconnaissance satellite. Indeed, Israel has been working on such a project for some time. However, even this does not provide an immediate or comprehensive solution, since it will take some time and its quality must yet be proven. Israel has also been pioneering the introduction of intelligence RPVs for use in combat formations. Reconnaissance satellites and long-range RPVs have the potential of greatly improving Israeli VISINT gathering, yet they are not a panacea for all intelligence problems due to the inherent limitations common to all VISINT tools (inability to read intentions directly or to know what is taking place in hideouts or under obfuscation). This was clearly evident in Israel's ongoing low-intensity warfare in Lebanon since the Second Gulf War.

The solution must focus on extending HUMINT sources too. These can compensate for the intrinsic shortcomings of VISINT, especially if the human sources have proper access to the higher echelons of the adversary. Israel, as we have mentioned, has certain fundamental handicaps in accessing information in countries such as Iraq, Iran and Libya, due to their tightly closed régimes and societies and due to Israel's lack of diplomatic relations as enjoyed by most Western countries.

Another issue that surfaced for the first time in the Second Gulf War was the extent to which Israeli intelligence depends on outside sources. This was most obvious in Israel's dependence on US early warnings of SSM launchings. It is not new for friendly intelligence organisations to exchange items of information or assessments, either occasionally or on a regular basis. Such an intelligence 'trade' is generally done, namely, on a give-and-take basis.

The situation in the Second Gulf War, however, was quite different: Israeli intelligence was totally dependent on the US in a specific realm. Indeed, no intelligence organisation can be altogether self-sufficient in its collection efforts or supply of information; it is only natural that gaps and missing pieces of information be filled in by means of free trade on an intelligence exchange. For Israeli intelligence to be completely in the dark and totally dependent with respect to a specific and crucial area of information was a new and unsound situation, which Israeli decision makers must take care to remedy.

Although Israel will always have gaps in its intelligence information, because its financial resources and other capabilities are limited, it must, nevertheless, never find itself in a condition where it lacks essential information. Israel's efforts to develop an intelligence satellite and long-range RPVs and other means are crucial in remedying such a situation. The need for such research and development was clearly manifest after the war, but must be kept well in mind as the peace process progresses, since the process is likely to diminish Israel's willingness to mobilise its limited financial resources to support ambitious defence projects.

These are all classical problems facing the Israeli intelligence community. In terms of overall defence doctrine, the problem is to acknowledge the need, to give priority and to allocate the appropriate financial, human and technological resources to intelligence. It stands to reason that the intelligence community will have to receive a bigger slice of the pie in order to cope more successfully with the many emergent complex problems facing it. One must bear in mind that, if only due to the rise in the weight of firepower and PGMs on the battlefield of the future, intelligence will have to provide combat forces and firepower with far more precise, as well as more extensive and detailed, real-time information.

ROLE AND FUNCTION OF IDF AIR POWER IN A FUTURE WAR

One of the principal questions raised by the Gulf War, and a question of great relevance to defence doctrine is whether, and to what extent, air power can decide a war. If it can, then it is in order to give the air force even greater priority among the IDF's pillars of power, with all the implications this has for the allocation of Israel's limited human and material resources. In other words, perhaps the balance between the various arms of the IDF should be re-evaluated. Notwithstanding the present, and correct, preference given to the air force, clearly a strong ground force is still required because, *inter alia*, enemy ground attacks cannot be fully halted from the air alone. Moreover, the Second Gulf War proved once more that one cannot achieve a decisive and comprehensive victory with air power alone. Aerial victory is essential in paving the way to overall victory but, in the Arab–Israeli context, it cannot suffice to produce a clear-cut or total victory.

The Lebanese–Israeli conflict provided us with two examples in 1993 and in 1996 which could consolidate the above mentioned observation. In operations Accountability (July 1993) and Grapes of Wrath (April 1996), the IDF extensively employed firepower in Lebanon in general and air power in particular, though the results were limited. Not that the IAF performed operationally poorly. Quite the opposite. The strategic problem was however, as had been demonstrated in the Second Gulf War, that firepower alone, including impressive air power, is not, and cannot be, sufficient to achieve a decisive victory.

An equally important question is whether changes should

be introduced on the operational level when employing IDF forces in battle; specifically, whether air and ground forces should engage the enemy successively or in parallel. IAF commanders, who, like others, marvelled at the employment of air power in the Second Gulf War, began to advocate emulation of this model of engagement with massive and protracted air operations until conditions are ripe for bringing in ground formations. To substantiate their view they argue that *with massive and longer air operations, the ground forces will have an easier battle, and, in particular, will incur minimal losses.* The obvious implication is that, in the initial stages of a war, the ground formations will not have to break through strong enemy fortifications and lines, which inevitably exacts a heavy toll. Moreover, once ground formations are brought into action the enemy disposition will have suffered significant attrition due to IAF pounding. Thus, essentially all the ground forces will have to do is to harvest the accomplishments sown by the air force. This may also mean that the land war may no longer have to be transferred immediately to enemy territory, as defence doctrine dictated in the past. Instead, this would only happen once favourable operational conditions have been laid.

As attractive as these arguments may sound, they have quite a few pitfalls, especially in view of the different conditions that pertained in the Gulf War as opposed to those that can be expected on the battlefield of the future in the Arab–Israeli conflict.

To begin with, in the art of warfare, in planning combat and preparing forces for war, it is a mistake to rely almost exclusively on one dimension of power – the air force – since failure of this force to deliver what is expected of it might be disastrous for the outcome of the war for a small country.

Secondly, in the Second Gulf War, the Coalition had hardly any political constraints or time limits dictating a rapid conclusion of the war. By contrast, it is well known that Israel would face a race against the clock in wartime. Engaging the air force alone for a protracted length of time might leave the IDF without any of the concrete achievements it might otherwise attain in a war. In such a scenario, the great danger is that IDF might not be capable of achieving the clear-cut victory that would be so important for further consolidating Israel's position in the region in the wake of a war and for buttressing the IDF's deterrence posture. Again, the IDF's operation Grapes of Wrath in Lebanon (1996) illustrated this observation.

Thirdly, despite the well-established supremacy of the IAF, the ratio of forces between Israel's air force and the Arab air forces is not the same as between those of the Coalition and of Iraq. Indeed, the IAF could fly much more than one sortie per plane per day (Israel could have flown six or seven times as many sorties as the US aircraft against the Iraqi SSMs).[4] The IAF could also carry more ordnance in battle (in the Second Gulf War the aircraft of the Coalition carried approximately one tonne on each combat strike),[5] and in general it could operate more efficiently than the Coalition aircraft, since it is more familiar with conditions in the local arena, has acquired well-established combat expertise, and is more willing to take risks for Israel's defence. The implication is, that despite being numerically small, the IAF's operational war output could match that of the Coalition's sizeable air force.

Although there is great substance to these arguments it would nevertheless be overstating the case to expect the IAF to be able to rapidly and decisively disable the air forces and air defence systems of its many enemies, near and far; the Coalition, after all, had to contend only with a single, isolated enemy.

Notwithstanding the above, the arguments of senior air force commanders should not be totally dismissed but, rather, should be given serious consideration and should be examined to see whether, and in which combat scenarios, they can be applied while bearing in mind the many and diverse constraints facing Israel. Air power, effectively and diversely equipped, perhaps reflects, more than any other component of force, the IDF's technological and qualitative edge. A massive, opening aerial stage, as suggested, can even provide a certain political advantage in that it is *cleaner* than a sweeping ground attack characterised by territorial conquest and inevitably followed by political *problems*. Moreover, even if a ceasefire is imposed by superpower intervention after the stage of aerial attack, if the air offensive is *strong and elegant* but still cuts off the *long-distance strike capacity* of the enemy, as well as other central pillars of his military power (such as the air force and air defences), then it could still leave a strong impact and yield important strategic gains.

Lastly, a few words are in order about the importance and future role of several aerial weapons systems that were prominent in the Second Gulf War.

First and foremost, attention must be paid to combat helicopters, whose importance in battle was clear to all before the war and was even more indubitable after it. For some time the IDF, too, has been making extensive use of fighter helicopters as its aerial arm, for tactical-operational purposes as well as strategic purposes – to provide a swift and flexible force that can be rapidly engaged to counter a dangerous surprise armoured attack on Israel. The IDF's policy, in the wake of the war, to expand its combat helicopter fleet and integrate it fully in land battle is definitely laudable. We should note, however, that bad weather is still an 'enemy' of air power and wise decision-makers should refrain from putting all their eggs in one basket.

Another area which has rightfully received emphasis within the air force and other arms of the IDF is the development and purchase of long-range RPVs for combat operations and intelligence missions. Such vehicles are needed for diverse military purposes, including possibly coping with SSMs in their initial stages of flight, thus complementing, or even providing a possible substitute for, the concept of ATBMs. Similarly, Israel should give serious consideration to developing and acquiring long-range radar, which could provide several minutes' advance warning of missile launchings and would be an integral part of the command and control system of the entire active defence programme. After all, there is no assurance that American satellites will always supply Israel with the information it needs (without charging a political price). Emphasis should also be placed on the development and acquisition of powerful electronic warfare systems which, in the Second Gulf War as well as Israeli wars, have proven highly effective for disrupting the operations of an enemy which, in combat, tends to function primarily by the book.

THE NON-CONVENTIONAL HAZARD

In terms of defence doctrine, the Second Gulf War raises two other challenging issues: first, the place of existing non-conventional weapons, primarily chemical, in a future war; and second, the weapons (primarily nuclear weapons) that can be anticipated in the region and ways of coping with them.

Chemical Weapons

As we have noted, it is no accident that in the Second Gulf War, in contrast to the First Gulf War, Iraq did not use chemical weapons against Israel or the Coalition. Still, there is no absolute guarantee that a megalomaniac ruler (we deliberately have not used the term 'insane') in the region will refrain indefinitely from making use of chemical weapons against adversaries of superior or equal non-conventional strength (as we observed earlier). It is equally wrong for a defence doctrine to be built on the working premise that employment of chemical weapons is henceforth possible in any armed conflict. A working premise that would be more relevant is that the use of such weapons is reserved for extraordinary scenarios, namely for national distress or extreme situations of military confrontation. In other words, it is reserved for situations in which the party using chemical weapons no longer has much left to lose, and when the end of the ruler himself, annihilation of his régime, or the collapse of the power bases of his state are at stake. For the reasons discussed above, and since Arab countries can tolerate greater overall losses and damage from the outset, it seems that in most respects – in terms of such factors as physical integrity and political prestige – the Arabs will not have a pressing need in the foreseeable future to resort to chemical warfare, unless some extremely exceptional circumstance develops.

Against the above observation, one could argue that there is nothing terrible about taking precautions for self-protection against chemical agents in the event that our working premise is wrong. However, in our opinion, when dealing with non-conventional weapons, an error of commission can be no less costly than one of omission. Moreover, the apparent shortcomings in protection against chemical warfare have a weighty military alternative in the offensive domain; and Israel is in no way entirely helpless. Quite the contrary, Israel's defensive policy against the chemical menace inherently weakens its overall security posture. Adopting civilian self-protection measures (such as gas-mask kits, sealed rooms and protected spaces) does more harm than good to Israel's image of national strength. The harm is not economic; rather, it is strategic and psychological, as we see from the protracted effects of the SSM launchings on Israel's national morale and self-perception. Mass psychology is an important factor in national security.

The grave error in the chemical defence policy, still being continued after the war, can be summarised in the following points: (a) Israel is granting legitimacy, albeit indirectly, for Saddam Hussein and other potential aggressors in the region to use chemical agents, even against civilian populations, in wartime; (b) since Israel is conveying the message that using weapons of mass destruction against a civilian, non-combatant population is not out of the question, it is also thereby accepting a change in the rules of warfare, dictated by its opponents; (c) Israel has correctly been stressing the importance of deterrence in preventing war, and the policy of protection against chemical warfare may signal a departure from this emphasis on deterrence.

It has always been clear that deterrence lies primarily in the ability to win decisively and to wreak retribution on the would-be aggressor. The crux of this capability has always been through offence, not defence. When the few are pitted against the many, the smaller party cannot defeat a multitude through defensive action alone. In the Second Gulf War, precisely when Israel's population was threatened with non-conventional weapons, Israel showed itself prepared for defence, and did not put all its efforts into stressing diverse offensive options. In so doing, regrettably, Israel diminished the credibility of its deterrence posture.

If the fear of non-conventional weapons is so strong, why were self-protection measures only taken against chemical warfare, and not also against biological weapons, which Saddam Hussein may possess and which others in the region might acquire? Was it only because the former, but not the latter, had already been used? In terms of the horrifyingly high number of possible casualties, the ease of employment, and long-term impact, biological agents are not a smaller risk – perhaps they are even a greater risk, than chemical agents. The Syrian régime seems to view biological weapons as a force equaliser, equivalent to nuclear bombs. Or were chemical precautions taken (even with the knowledge that these measures were not 100 per cent guaranteed) because of political considerations, to comfort the public and alleviate anxieties?

More importantly, a chemical attack on Israeli civilian centres could have grave, perhaps even dire, consequences. It is not a matter of a few fatalities, as in the conventional SSM attacks on Israel during the Second Gulf War. In terms of their cumulative effects, successful chemical attacks could claim hundreds, even thousands, of casualties each. Self-protection measures can reduce human losses but they pro-vide no guarantee of doing so, especially if there is a surprise chemical attack, or if 'persistent and penetrating' gases are used, or if weather conditions aid effective dispersal of the gas. It is doubtful that Israel, a small country exceedingly sensitive to casualties, could stand such a trauma. Even allowing that the defensive precautions adopted against chemical agents are in order (notwithstanding the debate in Israel about their efficacy) chemical protective measures are not necessarily completely effective, and they certainly do not provide a comprehensive response to this horrible threat and its collateral effects.

An alternative policy (for lack of a better option) is for Israel to adopt a pure deterrence posture, built on three levels: (a) Israel will not countenance a war involving non-conventional weapons, certainly not against a non-combatant population; (b) it will be prepared to take a calculated risk in not distributing chemical protection kits to its population; (c) notwithstanding the well-known difficulties of effecting a major departure from a previous policy, Israel must establish that it is unwilling, under any circumstances, to tolerate such new rules of the game. Likewise it should establish that it is unwilling to be singled out as the only state in the world, and certainly in the region, to provide all its inhabitants with means of self-protection (some of them quite embarrassing) against chemical agents, and it should adopt a comprehensive defensive policy.

Nuclear Weapons

Exposure of Iraq's attempts to acquire nuclear weapons generated waves of fear in the region on the one hand, and of admiration and a desire for emulation on the other. Regional aspirations for achieving a nuclear weapons capability, especially on the part of Iraq and Iran, pre-date the Second Gulf War by far, however. Nevertheless, in the wake of the war, acquiring a nuclear option has become quite attractive to several parties in the region. We refer primarily to Iran, but also to Algeria, Libya, Syria and Egypt. Indeed, Pakistan, a Moslem state on the fringes of the Middle East, probably has a nuclear weapon already. Many people believe that Israel, too, either possesses nuclear weapons already, or could attain a military grade nuclear capability instantly.

Given this setting, many analysts do not hesitate to predict a *nuclear era* in the region in the near future; and, to forestall this evil, they propose that Israel hasten to make peace with her neighbours in order to allay the danger of nuclearisation. In our opinion, both parts of this argument are equally irrelevant and untenable.[6]

Approximately eight states in the region are attempting to obtain nuclear weapons, but the most sinister threat is presented by Iran (since Iraq is now actually on the retreat in this respect), and next, possibly Algeria (which already has two atomic reactors at its disposal, one of which is not intended for peaceful research purposes). All the other contenders, especially Libya, Syria and Egypt, are many years away from actually attaining a military nuclear capability indigenously. The collapse of the USSR has evidently made it somewhat easier for wealthy countries in the region to obtain nuclear technology and weaponry but, in general, the aspiration to nuclearise is neither simple, nor inexpensive, nor capable of being rapidly realised. Nuclear weapons are likely to appear in countries on the periphery of the Middle East, most notably Iran, but, for all its deep-seated hostility to Israel, the Moslem fundamentalist state of Iran has been focusing most of its energy and interest on dangers in its immediate vicinity – Iraq, Saudi Arabia, the Gulf States, and perhaps also Pakistan, a nuclear state. Recently, the increased presence of the US (the 'big Satan') in the Gulf has also been a cause of grave concern to Iran, requiring a suitable response and deterrent on the part of Teheran.

A nuclear Pakistan, possibly followed by a nuclear Iran, could raise the fear of an *Islamic bomb* – a bomb which is possessed by a Moslem country and could also be handed over to the Arabs in their deep-seated conflict with Israel. The probability of such a scenario, however, seems slim. Any country that has obtained or created nuclear weapons (after long and painful efforts) and joined the exclusive *nuclear club* is unlikely to share its exceptional capability with other countries. Atom bombs are not a commodity to be traded, or bestowed as gifts – not even to close friends. *Friends* in such instances are trusted no more than enemies. Even Pakistan and Iran would not consider other Arab states sufficiently close friends to share such weaponry with them.

As with chemical agents, nuclear weapons will certainly be reserved solely for dire circumstances, when survival is at stake, and will not be employed for manipulative purposes. It does not seem that even deep-seated hatred of Israel will cause Arab states to break these basic rules, since in the non-conventional sphere we are dealing with extremely sensitive and dangerous weaponry and with threats that come down to questions of national survival. The fear of nuclear proliferation and of such weapons being passed around is also likely to be less relevant in the *new world order*, characterised primarily by the existence of a single superpower, by a tendency to moderate conflicts and abjure their solution through the use of force, and by the investment of great effort to prevent the proliferation of nuclear weapons and the means of their delivery (especially ballistic missiles).

Conflicts other than the conflict with Israel are the primary concern of those Arab and Moslem countries on the fringes of the Middle East that could pose a nuclear threat to Israel; and it stands to reason that the nuclear weapons in their possession, now or in the future, will be reserved first and foremost for deterrence against immediate adversaries and for ensuring survival. As for the Arab states in the heart of the Middle East, it is unlikely that they will obtain nuclear weapons or extensive nuclear capabilities before the end of the decade, if at all. Furthermore, if they should reach this point one day, it will still not give them an outstanding advantage over Israel, and it may even lead to the development of a local *balance of terror*. Not that this is much consolation to Israel, or that the rules pertaining to such a balance necessarily apply in the Arab–Israeli case, but it implies that, even in the Middle East, nuclear proliferation would not necessarily spell disaster. Ultimately one must distinguish between a potential threat – a nuclear capability in hand – and actual realisation of such a threat, which is reserved for most exceptional circumstances. In the nuclear sphere we are dealing with ultimate survival and even radical regional rulers must be aware of this.

Even if this assessment of the situation seems overly optimistic, Israel still has the option, and certainly the obligation, to make every effort, politically and militarily, alone or in conjunction with others, to prevent or forestall the introduction of nuclear weapons in surrounding countries. Political and operational intelligence efforts in this direction are especially relevant with respect to distant states, such as Iran, since Israel would find it difficult to repeat its independent military operation of June 1981, in which it destroyed Iraq's Osirak nuclear reactor. This approach could hardly be used as a regular, systematic method of removing distant nuclear threats. Moreover, obtaining plutonium from reactors is no longer the only way of achieving a military nuclear capability in the region. Another way, enriching uranium to weapon grade standard, can be implemented in numerous industrial-type facilities that could be concealed underground. It is also possible to build plutonium reactors underground provided an adequate cooling system is supplied, although this is considerably more complicated. In any event, in contrast to the past when a single, above-ground reactor was the primary nuclear target, now there may be dozens of nuclear targets, which cannot easily be attacked and destroyed, thus complicating the task of removing this threat.

The nuclear menace that might emerge from Iran is of greater and more direct concern to the US and the international community. By contrast, the military-operational aspects of removing the nuclear threat in states closer to Israel are relatively less difficult for the IDF. This might be one of the major reasons why these countries found it futile to embark on such an effort.

On the whole, it is not beyond the realms of possibility that Israel, with the help of its friends (especially the US) could yet prevent or forestall the development of nuclear weapons in surrounding countries. It is not simply a question of Israel's political or operational abilities, but first and foremost of conceptual awareness and of deciding to make every effort to prevent such a potentially ominous development. One certainly should certainly not conclude that a nuclear era in the region is imminent and inevitable. In fact, there have recently been several examples of countries being persuaded by international political pressure or inducements to forego their nuclear ambitions.

The argument that if Israel makes peace with its neighbours

this will save it from a nuclear era is oversimplistic. This claim appears primarily to serve a very biased political interest. As we have noted, the drive for nuclearisation in states such as Pakistan and Iran, and perhaps also Algeria and Libya, stems first and foremost from local controversies and rifts with neighbouring states. Therefore even the best peace accords between Israel and the Palestinians, Jordan, Lebanon and even Syria will not halt the efforts of countries on the fringe of the Middle East, especially Iran and Libya, to obtain nuclear weapons. Hence the nuclear danger affecting the region, and indirectly threatening Israel, will remain, irrespective of Israel's policy, the political process, or any rhetoric in this regard. One should not, therefore, use the threat of Arab nuclearisation as a whip to prod Israel in the political process or to demand that she pay an irrelevant and unacceptable price.

What should Israel do in the nuclear realm? Israel should continue its traditional policy of *not being the first to introduce nuclear weapons to the area, but also not being the second to do so.* Tiny and vulnerable Israel cannot afford to be confronted with a nuclear adversary without possessing similar weaponry. Likewise, any intellectual acrobatics on the matter, offering Israel an alternative formulation (such as disclosing nuclear capability in exchange for Israel withdrawing to its pre-1967 borders), are no more than exercises in futility.[7] Israel will not gain from exposing its nuclear capabilities.

Secondly, destroying the Iraqi nuclear reactor added an important dimension to Israel's policy, namely to use its long-distance strike capacity to forcibly prevent states that could endanger Israel from obtaining a nuclear capability. As mentioned, Israel must continue preventing and forestalling such a capability in the Middle East, especially in surrounding radical states. It is high time to understand that the danger of nuclear weapons lies far more in the nature of the state possessing this lethal weapon – in terms of the state's régime and social fabric – than in the hazardous nature of the weapon itself. Canada, for example, is not concerned, and rightly so, by the presence of a large nuclear arsenal in the

US, her immediate neighbour. Even countries such as Mexico, for that matter, are not much bothered. Likewise, European countries are not too frustrated by the fact that France and England possess rather large nuclear arsenals.

Thirdly, even if Israel were to agree to a regional nuclear weapon-free zone (NWFZ), provided the entire Arab–Israeli and regional conflict were resolved satisfactorily, general nuclear disarmament of the Middle East would still be neither simple nor realistic. As we have noted, the foreseeable nuclear threats to Israel do not stem as much from her immediate Arab neighbours, as from more distant Islamic states, which would not be induced to abandon their apparently justifiable policies of going nuclear simply because Israel had somehow settled her conflict with her immediate neighbours for the time being.

Developing Israel's nuclear potential was intended from the outset to guarantee the survival of this small nation against its many adversaries in the region, due to the immutable underlying circumstances of the conflict. It does not seem that these circumstances (especially the quantitative asymmetry) can ever change drastically, even with the signing of a peace agreement. The only cure to the nuclear challenge, as well as to the entire conflict, lies in a lengthy process entailing a revolutionary change in the values of Arab society and political culture. Israel will, therefore, have to be extremely cautious about its willingness to promote regional nuclear disarmament, even if a political settlement is achieved with some of its neighbours. On the other hand, Israel's neighbours need not be worried by a liberal, democratic country such as Israel having a nuclear potential. Like the rest of the world, they, too, know that Israel developed this capability because of its unique physical and historical circumstances and that it is only to be used as a last resort, and it is entirely up to them not to drive Israel into a corner. If Israel is not pressed, everyone may rest assured that it will not make use of its nuclear potential. In this sense, Israel will behave no differently from any other responsible power. If, on the other hand, Israel's adversaries cannot bear the fact that the Jewish state possesses a superior weapon, it is regrettably *their* problem and not Israel's.

In addition, the major Arab states and Iran are not entirely helpless *vis-à-vis* Israel, both conventionally and non-conventionally. Possessing other mass destruction weapons, such as chemical and especially biological weapons, is an enormous problem for a small and casualty-sensitive country like Israel. Thus, if they press Israel to dismantle its nuclear weapons, this is not so much for genuine fear for their survival as for prestigious pretexts, coupled with ominous strategic reasons, namely stripping Israel of its only assured remaining advantage.

Lastly, non-conventional threats also make it incumbent upon Israel to promote and develop its *active defence*, which operationally should be one of the central strategic responses to the nuclear threat of countries on the fringe and in the heart of the region. Specifically, it will provide a good way of countering nuclear weapons delivered by SSMs or aircraft. Even though no active defence system can guarantee total success (although the Arrow system is designed to come very close to doing so), the very fact of Israel having such a system can significantly deter a potential enemy in the region, since the high probability, indeed the near certainty, of Israel intercepting a nuclear or non-conventional attack in flight will greatly increase the ensuing threat to an aggressor's own survival.

THE IMPORTANCE OF TERRITORY AND STRATEGIC DEPTH

The SSMs that Iraq launched at Israel ostensibly served the arguments, voiced by politicians and others, that territory and strategic depth serve no purpose in the era of the missile. This claim was totally unfounded before the Second Gulf War and the war itself provided further solid evidence of the important connection between territory, strategic depth, and national strength and security. The great importance of territory and strategic depth in the Second Gulf War is highlighted in two contexts: the SSM threat and intelligence functioning.

The Context of the SSM Threat

As mentioned, SSMs only enhance firepower and do not introduce a revolutionary change on the battlefield. Prior to, and after, the Yom Kippur War (1973), the Arab states began emphasising SSMs out of weakness, due to their inferior air capability, displayed on more than one occasion when confronting the Israel Air Force. Arab states intended somehow to use SSMs primarily to counterbalance their inferiority in the air, so that they would not be utterly vulnerable in the face of IDF supremacy; but even the Arabs themselves still do not believe that SSMs have solved the problem or that they give them decisive superiority. Whoever exaggerates the threat of Arab SSMs and discounts the importance of territorial depth to Israel is ignoring the point of departure, which is an Arab sense of weakness that has not yet been dispelled. One should not, therefore, attribute to SSMs a power that even their owners do not ascribe to them, and certainly not in the context of the importance of territory.

The most conclusive rebuttal of the claim that the importance of territory is declining is, of course, the universally acknowledged fact that conventional wars are decided on the ground, and not by firepower. SSMs do increase firepower and make it easier to deliver; ballistic missiles can also cause damage and casualties, and even pose a considerable strategic, psychological problem. However, a SSM cannot conquer a single inch of territory. By contrast, land manoeuvres and troop ground movements involving substantial enemy forces can threaten one's vital territory and survival.

Three other fundamental arguments can be put forward in this debate. First, the same peculiar logic implies that whenever a newer, more advanced type of aircraft appears in the arena (such as the recently-introduced Sukhoi-24, which has a long attack radius of approximately 1,000 km and can operate in all weather conditions, not to mention even more sophisticated aircraft such as the Sukhoi-27, and others yet to come), strategic depth loses its value. Indubitably aircraft can be more menacing to the attacked party than SSMs, due to the greater load of ordnance they can carry (four tonnes per aircraft, as opposed to approximately one tonne for the original Scud missiles, and one quarter of a tonne for converted Scuds such as the al-Hussein), to their greater accuracy in hitting the target, to their ability to launch stand-off munitions from tens of kilometres away, and to other such factors. Yet no one has argued that the moment a more modern aircraft appears on the scene, the importance of vast territory and strategic depth suddenly diminishes – and rightly so.

Second, the dialectics of modern weapons development illustrates quite regularly that for every new weapon a counter-weapon is ultimately found. Thus a suitable response to the SSM, in the form of some anti-missile missile or even a long-range RPV, is likely to be introduced in the coming years. In the Second Gulf War the Patriot missile system already showed some positive indications for coping with SSMs, and its improved version (the Pac-3) is expected to be more successful at missile interception. The same will most probably occur with technologically advanced missiles specifically designed for intercepting SSMs, such as the Israeli Arrow and other ATBM systems being developed in the US. The argument that at present there is not yet a counter-measure against SSMs will have only temporary validity and provides no reason whatsoever for Israel to make crucial strategic concessions (namely, giving up important territorial assets) that it might regret for many years to come. Moreover, when a response to SSMs is found, will this specious argument be reversed – will secure borders, territory and strategic depth suddenly be important once more?

Third, the claim that strategic depth is of diminishing importance is almost surely politically motivated. Never have similar arguments been raised anywhere else in the region or the entire world. Some 1,000 surface-to-surface missiles were exchanged between Iraq and Iran in the First Gulf War, and some 45 Iraqi missiles landed in Saudi Arabia in the Second Gulf War, yet no one raised such an absurd contention in these cases. Nor has anyone in the world argued that borders should be shifted or that one should make do with less territory simply because of the threat of surface-to-surface missiles.[8]

The Second Gulf War actually underscores the importance of not giving up one's territorial depth. A major reason for Saddam Hussein not extending his invasion into the weak Kingdom of Saudi Arabia, or even into its important eastern province was that he feared he would be lost in its vast territory of 2.5 million square km. He was apprehensive of the close ties between the Saudis and the US; but little Kuwait also enjoyed similarly close relations with Washington, yet this did not save it from being invaded. We must assume that there was an additional factor deterring Saddam from attacking Saudi Arabia, and that was the vastness of its territory. Thus we may conclude that extensive territory and strategic depth are decisively important in deterring an adversary. They also provide a prescription for a successful outcome for the attacked party in an armed conflict. This is particularly relevant to a country such as Israel, having tiny territorial dimensions and being dominated to the east by elevated terrain.

Lastly, the Second Gulf War proved that Israel was, is, and will continue to be threatened from the east. The last time Iraqi forces joined in a war against Israel was in the Yom Kippur War, in 1973. The 20 years of relative quiet since then led some people to believe that this threat had diminished and hence they belittled its importance. The Second Gulf War, however, clearly demonstrated that the dangers from Iraq still exist and may even have become more threatening. This disproves the contention that there is less need for strategic depth because the threat from the east has diminished. Moreover, considering the additional potential danger posed by Iran, the importance of strategic depth to the east is, in fact, further enhanced.

Another valid point proving the importance of territory *vis-à-vis* missiles lies in the case of the Golan Heights. One rightly wonders why the Golan sector has been so quiet since 1974 and is not used by the Syrians to harass Israel, as they occasionally do, by proxy, in south Lebanon. The answer is quite obvious: because their capital, Damascus, is some 50 km away from Israeli lines *on the Heights*. This means that the presence of Israeli troops makes the whole difference. This very presence deters Syria from causing *any* flare-up on the Golan and probably also from initiating a war, which may immediately endanger its most strategic asset – its capital. Moreover, Israel's control of the Heights will probably also deter Syria from launching SSMs on Israel, as the IDF will be in a much better position, being capable of bombarding Damascus and its vicinity with artillery shells. This highly important territory creates an optimal balance of forces, which, in turn, will deter war and missile launchings. Keeping the Golan Heights is therefore an important lesson from the Second Gulf War.

The Context of Intelligence Functioning

The outbreak of the Kuwait crisis in August 1990 was a strategic surprise of the first degree, one more in a countless list of such surprises. One might conclude that strategic surprises are almost inevitable, even if intelligence gathering and output are improved. Even the airborne and spaceborne intelligence tools that the US had in abundance could not assure a timely advance warning; indeed, they were to no avail in preventing the US from being taken by surprise in the Kuwait crisis.

The main solution for small countries such as Israel, that, due to their circumstances, are prone to being strategically surprised, is not in the realm of intelligence, but rather in the realm of defence. The indisputable solution is to maintain extensive territory and strategic depth for defence. This is also the way to cope with initial military success by the adversary, which is inevitable once the enemy has seized the initiative and has attacked.

In view of the Second Gulf War, it is important to appreciate the true significance of strategic depth, especially in Israel's case. Possessing strategic depth is more than simply controlling sufficiently broad physical expanses for defence, which is always important and is an advantage in its own right. Strategic depth is significant in two other major respects. The first point, which has been well established, is that it is essential to begin defensive activity far from the vital areas of the state, which, if conquered or hit hard, would entail grave, if not disastrous, consequences. The second point, clearly brought out by the Second Gulf War, is that one should be able to recover promptly from a severe military setback resulting from an aggressor seizing the initiative and inevitably achieving initial gains, facilitated by his surprise offensive. Strategic depth, more than other military assets, can enable the defensive party to rapidly restore the *status quo ante* without suffering unbearable casualties and destruction. If this is true in general (as illustrated by the case of Kuwait), it is especially significant for a country such as Israel, with tiny territorial dimensions.

Given the fact that the Arabs have, and will always have, overall physical superiority, it is essential not to weaken any of Israel's three pillars of military might: manpower, weaponry and territory. Substantial erosion of any one of these will severely weaken Israel's side of the delicate strategic balance between her and the Arabs. The idea that one of these components can be traded off for another, strengthening one while weakening another, lacks foundation and is highly irresponsible. First, each of these components is essential and autonomous. Second, inroads have already been made in two of the three pillars – manpower and weaponry (the first due to serious rifts in political consensus and, consequently, lower motivation; the second due to insufficient financial resources and defence investment). If there is a further setback in the territorial factor, Israel will find itself seriously strategically disadvantaged, and this in turn will destabilise the region.

Israel must constantly maintain solid strategic assets, including strategic depth. In order to hold out in a hostile and unstable environment, a beleaguered state needs a critical mass of territory from the outset. Critical territorial mass is one of the basic pillars of defence which must not be relinquished if one wishes to assure survival. In time of war the value of alleged substitutes for territory, such as *security arrangements* and international guarantees, a foreign presence or buffer, demilitarisation, electronic sensors and other devices, airborne and hovering intelligence tools, and so forth, approaches zero, and, what is more important, their ability to prevent war is nil. The usefulness of these measures depends on the political will of a third party, which at times can be rather fickle. Israel should not therefore be overly dependent on others for its security and well-being. There are also tremendous practical difficulties in satisfactorily implementing security arrangements worthy of the name, including demilitarisation, force reductions and redeployment, that will allay the fears of parties like Israel. In short, there are no genuinely trustworthy defence arrangements that can serve in place of territory and strategic depth.

To sum up, developments in the art of warfare make strategic depth essential for Israel, now more than ever. Since firepower in general, and SSMs in particular, are likely to have greater weight in future wars, the issue of surprise attack has become even more acute. Even if advance and timely warning of ominous concentration of forces and war materiel could be provided under certain circumstances, such warning is much less likely to materialise in the case of hostilities erupting with massive firepower alone; and one cannot rule out the possibility of a war beginning with massive firepower before an offensive is launched by ground forces. Such firepower, if directed at Israel's centres of power, such as emergency store units, crucial road junctions, IAF airfields, radars and other valuable installations, could seriously disrupt Israel's orderly mobilisation for war. Moreover, if such firepower is delivered by thousands of artillery pieces, it could pose a severe problem for the IDF at critical junctures in time and place. It is thus essential for Israel not only to assure that enemy forces are deployed as far as possible from its vital areas, but also to preserve its strategic depth under all circumstances.

WAR OF CHOICE OR PREVENTATIVE WAR

Several remarks are in order on a traditional and universal principle of the doctrine of war and defence, which in Israel has ostensibly become less important over the past decade, especially since the Lebanese War (1982) namely, a *war of choice* or preventative war. For Israel, a *war of choice* refers to a situation in which the country must consider going to war because of a basic, grave and impending danger, a sinister threat which is in the process of developing but is not yet immediate or acute. In other words, Israel should consider launching a preventative war when it is faced by a grave threat to its security or well-being, which could worsen in the future, and not just when it is faced by an actual massing of enemy troops on the verge of attack. Preventative military activity is not only desirable when the knife is already at one's throat; the latter situation naturally calls for a pre-emptive (as opposed to preventative) action, the sense and justification of which is hardly challenged.

Recall the heated debate on the subject between Prime Minister Menachem Begin and his critics with respect to the Lebanese War. The late Prime Minister strongly advocated the principle of a war of choice, whereas his opponents believed that Israel should go to war only when actually attacked. Since much of the Lebanese war did not turn out well, *wars of choice* have appeared less advisable. Since then it has generally been maintained that it is preferable for Israel to go to war only when it has no other option – only when war is actually forced on it. Moreover, since the Arabs have demonstrated their ability to rebuild their military power relatively quickly after a war, and since they even improve their forces quantitatively and qualitatively, the impetus and rationale behind a war of choice seems to have declined.

The Second Gulf War illustrates a classical case of a war of choice. In this war the US went to battle without there having been any threat to its survival or serious danger to its security. Iraq did not endanger or pose an immediate or direct threat to the US or any other Western state. Yet, even after the Vietnam War and the fiasco of US intervention in Lebanon (1983–84), the US Administration was prepared to sacrifice soldiers and to risk going to war against a relatively powerful country.

Why did the US go to war? For two reasons, both of which clearly fall under the category of a war of choice: (a) to uphold an (international) principle, and (b) to safeguard certain national interests. The matter of principle found expression in US opposition to a tyrannical ruler and his reckless policies, specifically to a state that takes advantage of the weak and brutally threatens surrounding countries. Safeguarding certain national interests found expression in the US response to a potential threat to a friendly country – Saudi Arabia – in which the danger was twofold: jeopardising the steady flow of oil to the West (incidentally, of less importance to the US itself) and threatening the sovereignty and independence of an important ally. American national interest required that the US guarantee a central source of energy and safeguard the security of an important friend. Still, Iraq's invasion of Kuwait did not pose an immediate or direct threat to the security of the US proper, or even to its economy. Nevertheless, the US chose to embark on a war of choice, thousands of miles from its own shores, and in so doing it endangered the lives of many soldiers and risked many valuable resources, ostensibly for what had been termed *a gas station*.

The obvious question is whether a war of choice is only the prerogative of a superpower, implying that a small state such as Israel is not in a position to permit itself such a move. Is Israel not allowed to have national interests which it may defend even by the use of force? We hold that Israel certainly may go to war if in so doing it prevents a greater danger that might arise in the future, at a less opportune time. This is a universal principle underlying preventative war, resting on well-established traditions. Therefore, notwithstanding its well-known limitations, preventative war should not be flatly ruled out. There will, however, always be a problem of defining and characterising the threat, no matter how grave or basic it may be, and there will always be people prepared to argue, subjectively, that the danger is not so great or concrete that lives need to be sacrificed for it.

One can call to mind certain specific circumstances that Israel might view as justifying a preventative war, some of long standing and others quite new – for example, if a sizeable Iraqi force were to enter Jordanian territory, or if Syria were to make Lebanon a base for opening a potential second front against Israel, or if Syrian forces were to be significantly deployed in southern Lebanon. Threatening a vital Israeli interest, such as disrupting its maritime traffic, could also be considered cause to launch such a war; and the threat of SSMs being launched at Israel is certainly such a situation. Nor does it appear that Israel could accept the inhabitants of its northern settlements regularly becoming hostages to terrorist groups in Lebanon.

The fact that the US led a broad international Coalition in a war of choice should be borne in mind by Israel's political and military leaders. They must not view a war of choice or a preventative war as outlawed by an inviolable prohibition. This lesson for Israel from the Second Gulf War is no less important than the other lessons we have discussed here. Indeed, Israel twice faced a dilemma after the last Gulf War, when it launched two large-scale operations in Lebanon (Operation Accountability and Operation Grapes of Wrath). One might rightly question whether Israel's existence was at stake before it embarked on these semi-wars. The answer would be: on the one hand, the issue clearly wasn't survival and therefore a war was not needed; on the other hand, the strategic situation in northern Israel and south Lebanon was indeed unbearable, particularly when Israel's citizens and settlements became hostages to Hizballah terrorist rockets firing at will. The bottom line from both the Second Gulf War and other strategic circumstances is that war or large-scale operations cannot be restricted to a clear-cut no-choice situation.

NOTES

1. In this respect it is well worth reading Dan Meron's instructive article on the subject (which appeared during the war), 'If there is an IDF, let it appear immediately', [Hebrew] *Ha'aretz*, 14 February 1991.
2. Examples of the comments voiced include: 'If there is an Arrow, there will be no IDF', or 'The thousands of missiles the enemy will launch will wipe out Israel's defence budget.'
3. A. Levran, 'Israeli Intelligence in the Yom Kippur War', *Ha'aretz*, 2 October 1987; also cf. A. Levran, 'Surprise and Warning – A Study of Fundamental Intelligence Issues', *Ma'arakhot* No. 276-7, October–November 1980.
4. Cf. the remarks by former IAF Commander General Ben-Nun in *Tzevet*, No. 11, July 1992.
5. Cf. Commander of the IAF, *IAF Journal*, April 1991.
6. Cf. A. Levran, 'How to Tame the Nuclear Beast', *Jerusalem Post*, 1 May 1992; A. Levran, 'Nuclear Dilemma Grips Israel', *Defence News*, 20–26 April 1992.
7. For example, cf. the book by S. Feldman, *Israeli Nuclear Deterrence: A Strategy for the 1990s* (New York: Columbia University Press, 1982).
8. In the Cuban missile crisis in 1962, Washington brought the world to the brink of a nuclear war because the Soviets introduced SSMs in the US's back yard, although the USSR could have jeopardised American security in other ways. This underscores the importance of strategic depth in any context.

8

Principal Findings and Conclusions

To complete this study we present a brief summary of the main findings and conclusions.

(1) The Second Gulf War, a traumatic event for Israel, must not be swept under the carpet, but rather must be exhaustively studied in order to learn military and political lessons. This is essential for Israel for two reasons: (a) to enable appropriate policies and strategies to be formulated in the light of the lessons of the war, and (b) in order to read developments concerning post-war Iraq properly, especially the residual threat still emanating from that country.

(2) Even though the Second Gulf War and its aftermath have significantly reduced the risk of a fully-fledged Arab–Israeli armed conflict in the near future, this war has brought to the fore other grave threats for the more distant future, including a persistent build-up in qualitative weaponry, especially SSMs, which might be launched at Israel even from remote Arab and Moslem states. Another prominent long-term menace is the aspiration of some states in the region to acquire a nuclear weapons capability (not necessarily directly because of Israel). Iran appears most menacing, and Iraq would be equally dangerous should the international supervision and sanctions against it be relaxed. These two countries, as well as Libya, represent an ever-changing and expanding threat in the medium range.

(3) An important way in which Israel can counter the threat

of SSMs and nuclear weapons is through *active defence*, the essence of which is to develop and deploy a system of anti-missile missiles or similar measures. Israeli defence doctrine in the past functioned according to the well-known principles of deterrence and decisive victories achieved through offensive action. Today active defence must be added to this doctrine. Offensive measures alone will not suffice for Israel to cope systematically and efficiently with the dangers of firepower originating far from its borders. Moreover, Israel's air force, regardless of how successful it may be, is incapable of solving all the major emergent security problems facing Israel on its own. Active defence does not signal a revolutionary change in Israel's defence doctrine, which remains primarily focused on deterrence through offence, but rather reflects the need to adopt appropriate measures to cope with an acute challenge to the country's security.

(4) Active defence must not be developed at the expense of the traditional offensive deterrent approach, and especially not at the expense of air power. The Second Gulf War proved once more that appropriate air power can pave the way to rapid victory and that weakening this power can have dire consequences for one's overall military strength. Air power is certainly a requisite for coping with the most grave threat of all – a surprise land offensive. It is also advisable to re-examine the rôle of the IAF and its mode of engagement on the battlefield of the future in the light of the lessons learned from the air campaign in the Second Gulf War.

(5) Smart and stand-off munitions also emerged as prominent force multipliers, capable of enhancing Israel's qualitative advantage. They will be an essential factor in achieving a clear, swift, and rather inexpensive, victory in future classical or full-scale confrontations. Israel must marshal her economic resources in order to enable the IDF to progress in these three areas – active defence, air power and smart munitions. These avenues could

greatly reduce the risk of war in general, and could keep down losses and casualties if war were nevertheless to break out. In the final analysis, the economic burden of these measures will be far less significant than the alternative cost of being defeated or fighting a war that drags on.

(6) The IDF ought to promote new technology including a reconnaissance satellite and long-range RPVs. These are essential for visual intelligence enhancement and for coverage of actual and potential developments in nearby, as well as more distant, states. A reconnaissance satellite is especially important if political settlements are reached, since the latter are likely to limit direct VISINT coverage of the other party's territory by overflights and aerial photography. Although it is extremely important to improve the technical tools for gathering intelligence, one must not belittle the importance of HUMINT, whose absence in the Second Gulf War was sorely felt and has left its mark to this day.

(7) The fact that chemical weapons were not used in the war was no accident, despite Iraq's former intensive use of such weapons against the Iranians and the Kurds. It must be noted that even in those instances, Iraq followed an obvious pattern of self-restraint in employing chemical agents. Iraq did not use chemical weapons against Israel in the Second Gulf War because it was pitted against an adversary with equal, if not superior, strength, and in such a situation one does not hasten to resort to such horrible weapons, unless one is in an exceptional position of extreme distress.

(8) Israel's policy of protecting its inhabitants against chemical weapons during and after the war is ill-advised, since it signals acceptance of the possibility of this horrible, proscribed weaponry being used against a non-combatant population. It implies further that Israel no longer relies on deterrence through offensive power, as it

had in the past. It is not too late for Israel to revise its policy on this matter, and to make it clear that whoever attacks Israel with chemical weapons is assuming a grave responsibility.

(9) It is highly unlikely that Israel will be attacked by Iraqi SSMs in the context of occasional tests of power between Saddam Hussein and the UN. This is not necessarily the case because of technical reasons, such as Iraq not possessing an appropriate SSM arsenal or having difficulty operating its missiles, but is rather due to Iraq's present general military weakness and to constraints that have been placed on its strategic freedom of action.

(10) In view of the drive for nuclearisation manifest by some parties in the region, especially on the fringes of the Middle East, Israel must continue its established policy, one of whose principles is to prevent Israel's adversaries, near and far, from obtaining a nuclear capability. The political process is not sufficient to dispel Israel's fears of nuclearisation in distant Moslem states, such as Iran, Algeria and even Pakistan; but active defence (even if not 100 per cent guaranteed) could certainly help Israel cope with this menace too.

(11) Israel's overall potential for confronting the dangers threatening it lies, first and foremost, in its actual military capabilities, and not in the political process. This process may perhaps tone down the conflict with Israel's neighbours, but it cannot guarantee that the general dangers facing Israel in the long run will be eliminated. The only guarantee for Israel to consolidate her position and assure her survival in this troubled region is to remain a very strong country with effective military countermeasures for any major threat.

(12) The political culture of the region, characterised by persistent violence and the absence of true democracy, pluralism and accepted Western values, as attested by the many local conflicts (including the attempt to wipe

Kuwait off the map despite its peaceful, and even brotherly, relations with Iraq), gives reason to doubt that the political process will substantially reduce the level of friction between Israel and its Arab neighbours for a long time, or that it will bring Israel true peace. After all, two of the most bloody wars in the region – the First and Second Gulf Wars – were fought with no direct connection to Israel, although in the last one it found itself dragged into a remote armed conflict for manipulative purposes.

(13) One of the important lessons Israel should learn from the Second Gulf War is the very real danger that can be posed to the survival of a small state by a large, tyrannical, neighbouring power that covets its territory and wealth, despite ostensibly peaceful, even brotherly, relations that may have existed for years between the two. If such a fate befell Kuwait, it could certainly befall Israel as well. Israel, therefore, must not make the mistake of belittling the long-term dangers facing it, and it dare not trade off its inalienable pillars of military might for vain promises of peace and good neighbourly relations, which, in the mid-Eastern setting, are rather vacuous concepts. The Second Gulf War teaches that in the future Israel may again find itself victimised in inter-Arab hostilities to which it is not a party.

(14) Although deterrence has never been, and can never be, 100 per cent guaranteed, the failure of Israel's conventional deterrence of Iraq is especially telling with regard to its strategic equation with the Arabs. The debate over whether Israel's deterrence posture was weakened in the wake of the last war, and if so to what extent, is still open and cannot be answered definitively. Certainly Israel's self-restraint and inactivity in the war, although imposed by very specific circumstances, did not enhance its deterrence posture. This has been evident in its coping with terrorist activities perpetrated in southern Lebanon and by Palestinians.

(15) Israel will need every strategic asset currently in its possession in order to maintain its overall security and national strength. One such asset is sufficient territory to provide strategic depth for defence. The importance of this asset has in no way diminished, even in the era of the missile. This point has been reinforced by the lessons of the Second Gulf War. Strategic depth has become even more important because it provides the most appropriate response to sudden strategic surprise (which is almost unavoidable when the enemy decides to seize the initiative), and can help correct a situation in which the surprising party almost inevitably wins initial territorial gains. Strategic depth cannot be traded for *security arrangements* and *demilitarisation*, or airborne early warning devices (which, incidentally, proved to no avail in Iraq's surprise attack on Kuwait), since these are of limited value in preventing surprise or in promoting defence once war has broken out.

(16) By going to war in the Gulf, even though it did not face a critical danger or direct threat to its survival, the US illustrated that a *war of choice* or preventative war still has a place in strategic doctrine. The Second Gulf War should reinstate the traditional validity of a war of choice in Israeli defence doctrine. Israel should not be overly eager to launch such a war, yet neither should it categorically reject such an option. Its behaviour in the face of severe harassment from Lebanon since the last Gulf War proves this point to a great extent.

Index